MW00974489

MARRIAGE

WHAT'S THE POINT?

www.marriagewhatsthepoint.com

JESSE BIRKEY

?

MARRIAGE

WHAT'S THE POINT?

Revealing God's Purpose for Marriage

Marriage: What's the Point?
Copyright © 2010 by Jesse Birkey. All rights reserved.

No part of this publication may be reproduced, stored in a retrieval system or transmitted in any way by any means, electronic, mechanical, photocopy, recording or otherwise without the prior permission of the author except as provided by USA copyright law.

Scripture quotations, unless otherwise indicated, are taken from the *Holy Bible, King James Version,* Cambridge, 1769. Used by permission. All rights reserved.

Scripture quotations marked (NIV) are taken from the *Holy Bible, New International Version®*. NIV®. Copyright© 1973, 1978, 1984 by International Bible Society. Used by permission of Zondervan. All rights reserved.

Book design copyright © 2011 . All rights reserved.
Cover design by Richard Wilbert
Interior design by A&A Printing, Inc.

Published in the United States of America

ISBN: 978-0-578-08060-4
1. Family & Relationships, Marriage
2. Religion, Christian Life, Love & Marriage
10.03.16

Dedication

It is in all sincerity and humility that I dedicate this work to God and his glory. God was the inspiration, and I am just the vessel. I have no rights to this work. It is his.

Acknowledgments

I would like to acknowledge my beautiful and Proverbs 31 wife, Kara, for her pursuit of God's healing hand. One of the results of that pursuit is permission to write our story and allowing God to bring healing and hope to whomever he chooses. It has been a hard road to walk, and the fact that we are still walking and what God has done between us is a testimony of the glory of God. Thank you so much for your support and guidance. I love you!

I would like to acknowledge my friends and family who encouraged me along the journey. God used many of you to speak into my life in order to pull me out of the pit of hopelessness and despair. God used you to challenge my views and perspectives in this work and to refine them. Thank you.

I would like to specifically acknowledge my father. What a pillar God has used you as in my journey through tragedy and healing. God has used you to speak truth into my life. At times hard to hear truth but truth nonetheless. You never made a move to go with me down the path of bitterness but stood for righteousness. Even in the midst of my ranting, bitter spewing, hopelessness, and despair, God used you as a rock in my life. You were the kind of rock that didn't get in the pit with me but looked over the edge and extended your hand. As I reflect, I have not received any truth from you that did not majorly impact my life and relationship with God and Kara, and that is only a God thing. Thank you for hearing the voice of the Lord and being willing to speak. You laughed, cried, grieved, reflected, and much more with me. You have been a model of God's character and love to me. I love you!

Table of Contents

Foreword

I've known Jesse for about twenty years now, and if I were to come up with a list of top-ten adjectives to describe him, there's no doubt that the word *passionate* would make the cut. He is passionate about ideas, passionate about people, and most recently (and excitingly) passionate about God and God's heart for His people to know the freedom of real life in Him.

We've been hearing for a long time about the *marriage problem:* for many and complicated reasons, fewer and fewer marriages are "making it"—not just surviving but thriving. Jesse's desire is to try to get to the heart of the problem and to bring our focus back to God. At the core of this message, I hope you'll find what I did: that the love of God is not just a *remedy* for ailing marriages but is the *lifeblood* for any man and woman who have taken those vows to deeply and truly love each other.

God's passion goes far deeper than the surface. You'll undoubtedly see that Jesse's does too. And I know it's his (and

my) prayer that, in the pages to follow, you'll find that same
passion for life together as husband and wife.

—Marc Dejeu
Associate Pastor of Outreach Ministries
First Presbyterian Church
Beaver, Pennsylvania

Preface

We all have our reasons for getting married. I would imagine that most of us as we consider the reason we got married would come up with the hallmark answer of "because I love him/her." Others might consider that question a bit longer and come up with some different answers. We did not all get married for the same reason; however, I believe that most of us can come to the same conclusion that at the root of the reason for marriage, whatever it may have been, is selfishness instead of selflessness. I think this will become clear as you read.

God has created us with emotional needs. God has created us all with the same root emotional needs. These may look different on the outside as we all have our own ways of trying to meet those root needs. We take our expectations of how those needs will be met into marriage. The problem is that no matter how many marriage seminars you go to, how many books you read, and how many hours you spend in marriage counseling and therapy, your spouse is never going to be the one who can let you know how beautiful and awesome you are. Your spouse is never going to be the one who can let you know how appreciated you are or how deeply you are loved. Your spouse will never be the one who can let you know you are worthy. The only one who can satisfy these needs is God. Though you may have just said, "Duh! I know that!" do you really know it? Do you live like you know and believe it? I believe and pray you will find your answer as you read.

I started this project soon after some very significant emotional trauma. It is even now painful for me to write some of these things because it brings back very painful memories. The hurt is still very real and sometimes raw. Some of the statistics hit me hard because I am on the losing end of some of them. God has used this painful and terrible situation to bring incredible insight and revelation into what God wants our covenant of marriage and even all of our relationships to be like.

I have been in church my whole life but only recently discovered what it truly means to follow Jesus and be like him. It is a continuing work in progress. God has used the pain and tragedy in my life to bring revelation and transformation to my soul. I did not say that he is responsible for these things or that they even had to happen for me to learn, but nevertheless he did use the tragedy for amazing good.

I as a man have nothing that I can teach you. Human teaching is limited unless the Holy Spirit brings understanding and revelation to those who read. My prayer is that God's Spirit will indeed bring these words to life for you and give you greater understanding of what God wants for all of us and our relationships.

I admit that as a man I have the remarkable ability to get things wrong. I reserve the right to get things wrong from time to time. I do not present any of this as 100 percent error-proof fact. You, as the body or hearers, have the responsibility to test what you hear, measure it against what we know about God, and discern if it comes into alignment with his character. Even a strong conviction is just a strong opinion. So here we go.

Marriage: What's the Point?

A very well-known author and therapist has written a book on marriage. In this book he gives his opinion of what the ultimate purpose, or goal, of marriage really is. This is what he said:

> ... the supreme purpose of marriage is the union of two individuals at the deepest possible level and in all areas, which in turn brings the greatest possible sense of fulfillment to the couple and at the same time serves best the purposes of God for their lives.

I have a hard time understanding this statement, let alone digesting it. I do know it sounds a little magical to me. One of the questions I have is, Is this even attainable? The bigger question I have, though, is this. What happens when there is tragedy that breaks this union? What happens when there is betrayal, the death of a child, or the death of a spouse? What happens to this statement when the union is broken?

* * *

I remember it was a Wednesday night, and I was out fishing with my four-year-old son and a friend. I received a call on my cell phone, and I didn't answer it. After a little while I put my fishing pole down and went to see who had called. It was my wife, and she left a message. She told me I needed to be home by eight because a mentor of mine, Richard Mull, was going to be there. I was confused about why he would be coming over to my house. He had never been there before, and I could not figure out why he would be coming over this late. So we packed up and headed back in.

On the way back in to dock my friend's boat, I started to wonder if something was wrong. Kara had talked about some pain that she was going to ask the doctor about, so I thought maybe she got some tragic news from the doctor. I started to get nervous. So we got to land, packed up the car, and headed home. I called Kara to let her know we were on our way. I asked her if Richard had called her and asked to come over. She said no and offered no other explanation. So now I knew that she had called him and asked him to come over. I was now about twenty minutes from home, and the next thought that popped into my head almost sent me into a panic. The thought was that she cheated on me and wanted Richard to be there when she told me.

I don't know why, but I just knew that was the reason. The next twenty minutes were pure hell. Trying to drive on the brink of a breakdown. My son in the car with me. It was just terrible.

I called Richard when I was about ten minutes from my house, and I could hardly speak. I asked him if Kara had cheated on me. He did not answer yes or no but instead asked me to wait until he got to my house so we could talk. Well, that was enough for me. I lost it. It was a mixture of trying to catch my breath and sobs. I was very aware that my son was in the backseat, so I was trying my best to keep it together, but I was having a very difficult time. I just kept thinking this was not true.

I told myself there was a different reason he was coming over. I was going to get home and it would not be true and I would be so relieved. I told myself there was no way that she could do that to me. Not my wife. Not Kara.

Somehow I made it back to my house and pulled into the driveway feeling very numb. I could hardly stand as I let my son out of the car and followed him into the house. Kara was there sitting on the couch, and as we entered she took our son upstairs and put him and my daughter to bed. In the meantime, I had walked over to the couch opposite of the couch she was sitting on and sat down. I had a hooded sweatshirt on, and I pulled the hood up and over my face. I did not know what else to do. I felt void of everything. I felt like I had already lost everything. I just wanted her to come downstairs and give me the relief that I desperately wanted.

It took about ten minutes, and she came downstairs. Instead of coming over to me, she sat back in the spot she was in when we got home. She was silent. There was fear on her face, and she looked torn. We sat in silence for a minute, and there was no way I wanted to ask the question that I had to ask. However, I knew that I needed to ask it, so it came out like vomit. I did not even look at her, and my head was still under the hood when I asked with a shaky voice, "Who was it with?"

It was at that point she came unglued. She immediately started to sob and wail, and as she caught her breath between sobs, she was able to put together the choppy sentence, "Can't we just wait until Richard gets here?"

My response was louder now and less shaky as I told her, "No; who was it with?"

She continued to sob and break down and said, "You know him."

I did not know if I heard right, so I said, "What?"
She replied, "You know him."

There was not much thinking going on in my head; at this point I was just spitting things out. I immediately spit out the name of who I thought it was, and she nodded her head. That was all she could do because she had lost control in her brokenness. She could not even look at me. What followed was a rapid-fire string of questions on my part wanting to know what happened and what did not happen if there was anything. She either confirmed or denied my questions until I was out of questions for the time being.

I was lost in a world of unbelief and pain. My life was over. I have never known such pain. It felt like there was a jagged and rusty knife thrust inside me and was just ripping and tearing me apart. My world was crumbling around me, and there was nothing I could do to stop it. I wanted to vomit. I could not breathe, and my head was spinning. There was not much external emotion coming from me. I was in shock. I just could not believe what she was telling me. I wanted to call her a liar and tell her that I was not going to believe it.

I did the only thing that I could do. I got up and walked toward the door. She asked me in a panic where I was going, and I told her outside. As I opened the door, I could her hear telling me how sorry she was. I went outside to the driveway and just sort of collapsed. I just lay there not knowing what to do or where to go. I really needed help, and I was wondering where Richard was and what was taking him so long to get to my house.

A couple of minutes passed, and at one point, I heard the front door open and footsteps on the driveway. I did not turn my head, and just as quickly the footsteps went back to the house and I heard the front door close. I assumed Kara had come out to see if I was still there.

I felt like I was in a movie. It did not feel real. This is the kind of thing that happens to other people and not to me. I decided that it might be better to get up and start walking down the street, and so that is what I did. As I was walking, I had the urge to start running and to never stop. If I could just run away, the pain would stay back there. I could start a new life. I did not have to stay with her. Jesus gives an exception for divorce. He said that it was permissible if there was unfaithfulness.

As I was pondering these things, I looked up and saw Richard's van coming down the street. I stumbled over to the passenger side and fell in. I looked at him, and the emotion started to come. I started to sob, and I told him that I did not want to go back there. I told him that I did not have to stay. I repeated that. I was so broken. He pulled into my driveway and talked to me for a couple of minutes. He asked me if I was ready to go inside. I said yes, so I followed him inside and collapsed on the stairs. Kara was sitting in the same spot that she had been in. When she saw Richard, she lost it again and just kept apologizing.

I felt myself get angry. I fired at her, "How could you do this to me? Do you realize that you potentially destroyed your family and there is a good chance you destroyed someone else's?" I could feel myself losing control, and I knew that I had to stop. The amazing thing was that I could stop. Praise God for that.

I stood up and went to the bedroom and started to pack a bag. I planned on going to my parents to spend the night. Richard came in the room and talked to me a little. He asked me if I wanted to hear what God was saying. I said, "*No!*" Honestly I was not interested in what God had to say at that point because I knew that he was going to ask me to do something that I really did not want to do. In the year prior to this I had been delivered from emotional bondage that kept me from feeling for eight years. It was an emotional wall preventing me from really connecting intimately with anyone. Well, I could feel that old familiar wall trying to come back up. I had to will it down. However, it seemed very appealing.

Richard then told me that he knew I was going to walk through this well. I looked at him and said, "What is well?" He did not have an answer for that. That was very encouraging to hear. He had enough confidence in what God had done for me up to that point that he could say that I was going to walk through this well.

After a couple of minutes Richard left the bedroom and prayed with Kara. I was alone in the bedroom, and I just did not know what to do. After a while Richard left, and Kara came into the bedroom shaking and crying. I could no longer hold myself up, so I just dropped to the floor. Kara came over and collapsed in front of me. It was at that moment I began to really know that I was not the same person I had been a year ago.

* * *

Marriage, what's the point? Have any of you ever asked that question before? I never did. Like most of you I thought I had a pretty good reason for getting married. Actually, a handful of what I thought were good reasons. Some of those reasons I consciously recognized, for example: because I love her, because I want to share my life with her, because I am supposed to get married at some point, right? Another obvious reason is that I wanted to have kids. I wanted to grow a family.

However, there were also some not so obvious reasons that I had. These reasons went unnoticed by me, but nonetheless they were there and very real. Through the process of healing past emotional wounds, God revealed to me other reasons I desired to be married, reasons born from pain and ungodly belief systems. These were some very personal and deeply rooted issues. These issues had roots in the fear of rejection. I wanted to be accepted. There were also roots in how I didn't like myself very much. In fact, I would say that I did not like myself at all. I wanted to feel good about myself, so I married a beautiful woman. These things run very deep, and they are, in reality, a very common scheme that the enemy likes to deploy. It is effective. If it was not, Satan would not use it as much as he does.

I grew up in a typical home. Well, now that I think about it, my childhood home was very atypical. I had two parents in the home, and they were both my biological parents. That is rare these days. My parents are still married today after thirty-some years. That is also rare these days. My father was a pastor, and my mother was and still is a nurse. I was raised to know and love God, and I am very grateful for that.

My parents were not super strict, and I am also thankful for that. There is a stereotype for families in which the father is a pastor or minister. We think that they never go out and only watch G-rated movies. They certainly never drink alcohol or smoke. They hardly even watch television, and if they do, it's only religious shows. If you ever screw up or get in trouble, you most certainly get the Bible shoved in your face or maybe hit in the head with it. I am not saying that alcohol consumption went on in my house or that shows were watched that were ungodly ... well, actually I am.

Hold on now, the alcohol was rare and always in moderation, as far as I know, and the shows were, well, funny. I was allowed to watch R-rated movies with my parents and by myself when I was sixteen or so. I had a lot of freedom.

I don't remember watching many, if any, religious shows on TV. Well, I take that back. Watching the Kansas City Chiefs play football on Sunday afternoon was a pretty religious activity. I was always allowed to go out but had a very lenient curfew. I had earned trust in that area. Suckers! Just kidding.

The family dynamic that I grew up in had its flaws, but it was good in the sense that it taught me that families stay together and work out problems. Divorce was never an option for my parents. Problems were always going to get worked out. That does not mean there were never any colorful and animated "discussions" but that they were resolved. My parents were two walking examples of forgiveness. That's how it appeared to me, and that is what stuck most significantly with me. While families crumbled around me and my childhood friends came with reports that their parents were getting separated and divorced, mine stayed together.

There was a lot of emphasis on communication in my house. No one was allowed to give anyone else "the silent treatment." Thinking back, being silent a little more would have saved me some trouble at times. Words occasionally, well frequently, have the tendency to make things worse, especially for me. Being forced to communicate really taught me how to work out problems. I learned how to use "feeling statements." My father pointed out that I did not have the complete understanding of them when one night I told my older sister, "I *feel* that you're an idiot."

My parents have said that they don't regret getting married but readily admit to the many problems and issues they have had over the years. Even though they never tried to hide their problems to present a "perfect" image, I still grew up to have an unbalanced view of marriage. It wasn't that I thought my marriage wouldn't have any problems; it was that in my spirit I believed I was above many of them. It wasn't until I married my wife, Kara, that the problems I thought I was above became a terrifying reality.

I met Kara the summer of 2001. She was one of my younger sister's best friends. She was over at my house hanging out with my sister when we interacted for the first time. I was home from college for the summer, and I thought she was the hottest thing I had ever seen. Well, that fall I went back to school. I came home the following spring break and we interacted more. There was a connection. My younger sister was less than pleased at the situation, so there were no dates during that time but plenty of talking and flirting. She was everything that I was looking for and wanted. She was fun and easy to talk to and beautiful. She was also a born-again Christian. That was very important to me. When I was on my way back to school, I received two e-mails from Kara, and the rest is history. I came home from school for good in May of 2002. We were engaged in November and married less than a year later.

I was twenty-one when we got married, and Kara was only nineteen. The running joke is we would have had some alcohol available at the reception, but if the bride is not old enough to drink it, no one can. It was a beautiful wedding, and Kara was radiant. It was a pretty big wedding, which was great for us because we knew that most every person that was there was bringing a present or a card with money in it. I mean because we were happy to see all of our friends and family. My father gave the meditation, the short version as requested by me, and Kara's pastor gave the vows and pronunciation. I gave the kiss to the bride.

Never throughout all of this growing up, school, dating, engagement, wedding, and marriage did I ever ask the question, "What's the point?" The thought never crossed my mind. If I was going to ask any question related to that, it would have been "What's the point of this beautiful and fun-loving girl, Kara, marrying me?" That is pretty messed up, and I do not think that way anymore, but I was very aware of all the "garbage" I brought into the marriage. I put Kara through a lot of pain because of my struggles. The three main problems were struggles with pornography, gambling, and the inability of me to open up emotionally. Both of us brought garbage into the marriage, but mine seemed like a mountain and it created an inability to see the issues she brought to the table. The result was the belief system that she is perfect and I am scum. The implications of this made me exist in a marriage where, in my mind, all I ever did was hurt her. It held me in constant shame, guilt, and condemnation. However, asking the question "What's the point?" on my end? Naw, I had plenty of reasons.

* * *

From Kara:

Like Jesse, I also grew up in a "normal" family. My parents are still married; both are Christians and have always provided everything my siblings and I needed. I feel extremely blessed to have been raised in a family where abuse, alcoholism, or any of the "biggies" were not an issue. Needless to say, my family was also not perfect. No one's family is and will never be. You simply do the absolute best you know how and pray that God will be at the center, right?

Growing up, I did not have a single career ambition. What did I want to do with my life? All I have ever aspired to be was a wife and a mommy. This was modeled by my mom, who was a stay-at-home mom for most of my childhood. I, to this day, really do not have career ambition and feel that as long as God allows, I will be at home for my family as much as possible. I praise God that he allowed me to have my dream.

Was it all that I had imagined? Not a chance! I visualized myself in a perfectly spotless house, with perfectly respectful children, with a perfectly in shape little body, running around in an apron and high heels, and providing four-course meals every night for dinner. In case you are wondering … this is *not* reality! Did I ever ask, "What's the point?" No, but maybe I should have because then I may not have had such a skewed idea of what marriage is really all about.

∗ ∗ ∗

I did some research on the Internet to find out what people are saying about marriage. Here is some of what I found.

> An opinion on marriage. Well, let's see, I was married for 13 years and then was told that she didn't need me anymore. She told me that she had a good job with good benefits and she had no use for me anymore. So, I gave her what she wanted, her freedom. But really, marriage is a good thing. I wouldn't have traded it for the world. Sometimes it gets a little hectic, trying to bring two minds and opinions into one world, but that is easy to overcome. Marriage is a job, it's something you both have to work at to keep it going. You can't have one person doing everything while the other person is doing

absolutely nothing, otherwise it'll never work. There is a lot of give and take, but I think it's worth it. Even though mine didn't work out the way I wanted it to, I planned on being married for life, I do believe that it was the best thing that ever happened to me. Whether or not I would do it again, well, that'll have to come in time.

This person was obviously hurt badly by his wife. He says some things in a matter of fact way, but the pain seems to run deep here. After thirteen years, his wife just decided that she does not need him anymore. Marriage is a job? It's an opinion many of us would share. "Marriage is hard work" is a common statement. This person states that the marriage was the best thing that had ever happened to him, but after thirteen years and then an ending like that, I bet he was asking himself, "What was the point?" frequently. Here is another:

> Its a lovely concept … created thousands of years ago, at a time when life expectancy didn't surpass 30 … "till death do us part" had a much different meaning back then.

This is an interesting statement. It shows commitment at least until the age of thirty. This commenter also refers to marriage as a "concept." How can we hope to put all that we need to put into marriage when we just view it as a concept? Here are some more:

> I think marriage is like a bank account, you put in and you take out, you put in and you take out … and after awhile you lose interest :) freedom is a good feeling.

> Its a contract to protect unborn children and to some extent property. There are tax breaks associated with it, and the government encourages it. Quite a few people are forced to lie, predicting impossibly that they will stay together for life. Arranged marriages have a higher success rate as our western culture bases marriage on "falling in love" rather than growing into it.

It is not always forever. Only diamonds are. I believe that instead of saying "I'm going to love you forever", we should instead say, "I'm going to love you for as long and as best as I can." Love like any other emotion is transient. We shouldn't be held accountable if we can't love someone forever.

Marriage is a legal prison. The law sees us as one so I can't sue him for stealing my CC check & forging my name, the tax law believes I have shared his income (which I haven't) and then penalizes me with zero deductions because my husband owns a house and I don't. Legally, someone can turn marriage into date rape. So long as he doesn't hit you, your marriage is okay in the eyes of the law. This was not a real marriage—a partnership of mutual respect and care. It was a license to steal.

… and then the ever popular:

Don't do it!

Seriously! Someone really wrote that last one.

Now we have no idea if the people who posted these opinions ever asked the question "What's the point?" but they certainly seem to be asking that question now. You might think the responses here are slanted and they must not have posted the responses in favor of marriage. Let's do some reminiscing.

Can you think back to when you got engaged and people found out? Were the responses positive or negative? Men, I am speaking to you in particular. Get past the initial congratulations of your good friends and remember the jokes that came after that. For example: "Why would you want to give up your freedom?" and "Why would you want to have sex with the same person for the rest of your life?" How about "Are you sure that you want to do this?" Even though most of these are said in a joking way, they are still negative and do come from the overall sense of doom that follows marriage. It is not hard to understand that sense of doom when you look at the statistics. Marriage is the punch line of jokes, the bitterness-soaked spewing of broken individuals, and the subject of, only God knows how many, self-help and counseling books. Marriage has given careers to therapists and divorce lawyers and headaches to the economy. Let's not forget the show themes that marriage and the antics that go on have given to Maury Povich and Jerry Springer. With all of this, add the gross amount of cheating and affairs that go on, and you have to be wondering, *Does anyone take marriage seriously anymore?*

Here are some percentages for you, 50 *and* 60 *percent. Fifty* is the percentage of women that will have an affair at some point in their marriage, and *sixty* is the percentage of men that will have an affair at some point in their marriage. In the life of your marriage, there is an 80 *percent* chance that someone is going to cheat. This is taken from the *Journal of Couple and Relationship Therapy.* Per this journal these are doubled numbers from ten years ago. I would think that probably 50 percent more people are actually admitting it. People, this is disgusting. It should cause your stomach to turn. It does mine, and I get upset and frustrated.

There are plenty of books written on the subject of why people cheat. What's more irritating is that those who have an affair are likely to have another one at some point. Or the other individual in the marriage will have an affair for revenge, out of hurt, or whatever the reason. It is possible for God to restore a marriage wrecked by unfaithfulness. I think that we all would agree on that point. That statement is good in theory. Do you personally know a couple in which there has been unfaithfulness and the marriage survived? If it did survive, are they really still happy, if they were happy at all?

Many times we survive pain and trauma on the outside but it has destroyed us on the inside. Think about it. Are you really surviving if you are unable to trust your spouse, constantly hating him/her, feeling permanently rejected, telling yourself you couldn't do any better, and feeling trapped knowing divorce would damage your kids? Is erecting the emotional wall, pushing away the pain, and pretending it never happened a better alternative? Maybe you think it is, but I know from experience it won't be the answer you hope it will be.

Here is another uncomfortable statistic:

- 50–60 percent of marriages end in divorce, according to multiple online sources.

Divorce statistics by religion:

- Jews 30 percent
- Born-again Christians 27 percent
- Other Christians 24 percent
- Atheists, Agnostics 21 percent

Let me get this straight. Not only are the numbers for divorce staggering, but Jews and born-again Christians, or evangelical Christians, top the list for divorce. Born-again Christians have a higher rate of divorce than atheists and agnostics put together according to this online source. Unbelievable! On top of that, I hope that you are not a firefighter, police officer, or in the military because the percentage of divorce climbs even higher for people involved in those careers. It climbs up near a staggering 85 percent.

After all these statistics and numbers, you have come to realize that the chance of your marriage lasting has come down to a coin flip as far as the world is concerned. Add in all of the pain and devastation that comes with divorce, and we have to be wondering, *Why even get married at all?* What is the point of getting married only to have a much better than fifty percent chance that there will be indescribable pain and suffering?

Some of you may be thinking that you are or will be on the winning side of those statistics. If you are, then praise God. If you stay that way, then praise God even more. However, expectations are dangerous things and promise to bring disappointment and letdown. It doesn't matter if our expectations are positive or negative, we are going to be let down. No one can meet our positive expectations all of the time, and it appears most of us are experts at meeting the negative. Consider this point for a moment and decide if there is truth in it.

In the pages ahead you are going to find the understanding and revelation my wife, Kara, and I have discovered together. The reasons we get married described in the pages ahead all hold significance for us. You have heard and will continue to hear from my wife at different points throughout, offering her perspectives. Part A is going to sound very pessimistic. Well, actually it will be very pessimistic, but that is only part A. Part B will place before you a solution and let you in on what we believe the real point of marriage is as defined by God, what he expects, and what he has always wanted it to be. There is a point to marriage, and it is beautiful. Unfortunately we have to clear out all the reasons that only bring hurt and pain.

I also want to state here that I reserve the right to be wrong. I have been wrong once or twice in my life. The following pages are my opinions and what I believe God has impressed upon me in this season of my life. If you agree with me, then great, and if not then that is okay. Over the course of this book, I am going to bring up some issues that may make you want to immediately deny and dismiss. I know this because as we have discussed this book in our small group, there have been many debates, and things have, at times, become a little heated. All I am going to ask from you is an open mind and a willingness to ponder deeply before dismissal. So here we go with the reasons that we have become comfortable with as to why we get ourselves into this thing we call marriage.

Trust, Loyalty, and Dependability

Who do we trust? Who have we determined to be trustworthy? Three people come to mind—God, our spouses, and ourselves. Even if we have determined our spouses and God are untrustworthy, we somehow still believe that we are trustworthy. Most of us would say that the ability to trust our spouses is an essential part of our marriages. We say we can't have marriages without trust. However, 80 percent of us have or will experience betrayal (unfaithfulness), and most of us don't trust our spouses enough to be completely intimate and vulnerable. It's ironic we would say we can't have marriages without trust when most of us don't trust our spouses at all. As far as God goes, we have not the slightest clue what it means to trust in God. This is also ironic since he is the only one who is completely trustworthy all of the time.

I believed that trust had to be a part of my marriage, but

ife. Because of rejection, pain, and
life, there was an inability in me to
rability. My biggest fear was that
s a tormenting fear. I have come
..y to trust will undoubtedly spill
ur our lives. I came to understand that I
wnat it means to trust in God. I was trusting God
..u keep me comfortable in my standard of living. The fact
that God's standard of living can be much different than ours
wasn't even on my grid of understanding. What I have come to
understand is the three people we feel are trustworthy aren't as
trustworthy as we think. Yes, I included God in that because
our idea of what it means to trust in God is so messed up and
misunderstood—we don't really trust him at all.

Let's talk about us. We are so trustworthy, right? When
everyone else around us fails, at least we can trust and depend on
ourselves. Let's evaluate that. Have you ever let yourself down?
What if you're an alcoholic and you find yourself at a bar with a
double shot of your favorite liquor in front of you? Add to the
mix that you just got dumped by your girlfriend or boyfriend, or
your wife or husband just left you. Do you trust yourself not to
drink in that situation? Let's say you are a compulsive gambler
who finds an extra hundred dollars in your pocket while passing
a casino. Do you trust yourself not to stop and gamble? Let's say
you are an individual who has failed many times over the course
of your life. You have not felt loved at home or have been fired
from jobs. You have been constantly looked over when promo-
tions were handed out, and you never get a pat on the back. Do
you think you can trust yourself not to fail if and when given
an opportunity? Say pornography is a struggle for you; it's 1:00
a.m., and you're the only one up with the computer. Do you
trust yourself not to look? The drug addict who wants so badly
to stop being destructive gets paid. After failing so many times,
do you think he/she trusts they will not buy drugs? You are a
compulsive shopper who needs to buy groceries but on the way

passes a great sale. Do you trust yourself not to stop and cut into the grocery money? Your spouse says he/she is unhappy. Do you trust yourself to make him/her happy? Do you trust yourself to be a good Christian? Do you trust you can follow the commandments of God?

If I am going to get honest and look back on my life, I am the last one I would have trusted. I did not trust myself to be able to resist pornography. I did not trust myself not to gamble. I didn't trust I could provide for my family. I didn't trust myself to be alone with another woman. I did not trust that I could be a great father. I did not trust I could be a great husband. I could not trust I could be a great firefighter and paramedic. I could not even trust that I could be a good Christian and that God would be pleased with me. I didn't trust myself not to spend money on things I wanted regardless of what our family needed. I didn't trust myself to be able to open up emotionally to my wife. I certainly didn't trust in my ability to make her happy. I had no trust in myself not to fail. About the only thing I could trust about me was that if I were coach of the Kansas City Chiefs we would never lose. The funny thing is, years ago I would have said I was definitely trustworthy.

What I am sharing are things I have realized looking back. These are pretty messed-up views, and I was in bondage that I am no longer in today. I don't have trust in and of myself, but I no longer hold on to negative views. God took me through a lot of healing in that arena. So I do not trust in myself. Praise God for that because Paul states that we shouldn't.

> But we had the sentence of death in ourselves, that we should not trust in ourselves, but in God which raiseth the dead.
> 2 Corinthians 1:9

> Do ye look on things after the outward appearance? If any man trust to himself that he is Christ's, let him of himself think this again, that, as he is Christ's, even so are we Christ's.
> 2 Corinthians 10:7

Trust in the LORD with all your heart and lean not on your own understanding; in all your ways acknowledge him, and he will make your paths straight.

Proverbs 3:5–6 (NIV)

So go ahead and get honest with yourself. Can you really trust yourself for anything?

At least our spouses are trustworthy, right? We may have realized that we are not that dependable, but surely we can trust our spouses. Let's evaluate this next. Has your spouse ever let you down or disappointed you? Of course he or she has. You may be thinking of a little example of a time that your spouse let you down. Not that it is insignificant, but the sorrow was not long-lasting. So let's ask the question, "Can you trust your spouse not to cheat on you?" Ooh. Now we are going somewhere. To those of you that said yes, how can you be sure?

Can you be assured of your spouse? How can you be if we are all imperfect people? The only one, and I mean only one, that can accept the trustworthy title is God. What you are really doing is *hoping* that your spouse will never cheat on you. Let this sink in before you read on.

For those of you married to an addict, can you trust the drug, porn, alcohol, food, money, shopping, sex, gambling, and whatever else addict not to get their fix? "Well, they said they would stop." Okay, how many times does it take before that line becomes meaningless? Is there any real trust in a relationship like that?

Can we trust a spouse who can't even open up to us emotionally and intimately? There is no one on this earth, your spouse included, that we can have assured reliance in. In us character fails, ability fails, strength fails, and truth fails. Anyone who has been married for five years knows this well. Heck, even if you have only been married for one year, you have probably experienced these things failing in one way or the other. "Well, I just do not accept this," you say. Maybe you're thinking that

God has made some kind of provision for us to be able to put trust and faith in people. Somehow we have separated in our minds people and our spouses. We seem to have put them into separate categories. We think that we cannot trust people but our spouses are a different story. Let's see what the Bible has to say on the subject:

> Trust ye not in a friend, put ye not confidence in a guide: keep the doors of thy mouth from her that lieth in thy bosom.
>
> Micah 7:5

It may surprise you to know that the Hebrew word for *friend* used here means an *associate* (more or less close): "brother, companion, fellow, friend, husband, lover, neighbor." That covers just about everyone, and here is the reason:

> For the son dishonoureth the father, the daughter riseth up against her mother, the daughter in law against her mother in law; a man's enemies are the men of his own house.
>
> Micah 7:6

This paints a pretty bleak picture, does it not? A man's enemies or adversaries are the men of his own house. So who can we trust? Read on:

> Therefore I will look unto the LORD; I will wait for the God of my salvation: my God will hear me.
>
> Micah 7:7

Is that okay with you? It sounds like it has to be. Can we get the fulfillment we crave by only trusting in God? Take a moment to consider this and be honest. If everyone were to abandon you, leaving you alone in this world, is God enough for you?

That leads us into the last person we say is trustworthy, God. He is the only one who is trustworthy all of the time, but that doesn't mean we have any idea how to trust him. Let me say this carefully, and please don't misunderstand what I am saying, *our perception of what trust means makes God untrustworthy.* My old perception of what trust meant made God untrustworthy and unreliable to me.

What does our trust in God look like? Are we viewing trust in a way that says "I trust that God will keep me in the same house that I am in now" or "I trust that God will keep me employed so that I can meet all of my financial needs" or even "I trust that God will keep me and my family from all harm, pain, and suffering"? Essentially, we are saying we trust God to maintain our idea of what a standard of living should be. If we are able to maintain it, we say we are blessed, but if we can't we are being punished and just need to pray harder. God forbid we should lower our standard of living willingly as circumstances develop. If this is what we are saying, we need to reevaluate our perspective of trust.

I have noticed something about God. He can, at any time, call you to pick up your family and everything that you own and move to the other side of the country or even the other side of the world. He can also take you through a very difficult time of learning to trust in his provision, which does not depend on your own strength or skill set. I can almost assure you God's idea of what you need is very different than your idea of what you need. God will also allow all kinds of pain and suffering for the purpose of refinement and growth. Let me be clear here that God is not the author of pain and suffering. However, God will allow Satan to bring consequences to us based on the choices we make. It is not important to God to maintain your standard of living. It's important to God that you trust him completely.

This is why we cannot trust God the way that we understand trust. We have not been trusting in God. What we have been doing is *hoping.* Now let me say something here because I know that hope instead of trust implies an uncertainty. We can hope in God and be okay with that. We can hope in God for the things that we desire, but beyond that we can trust that he will provide all of our needs and keep his promises. We know and believe that God will keep his promises, but we hope for different things a lot of the time. Let's take a look at the examples I gave earlier, but I will replace *trust* with *hope* as it should be. "I *hope* that God will keep me in the same house that I am in now." Or "I *hope* that God will keep me employed so that I can meet all of my financial needs." Even "I *hope* that God will keep me and my family safe from all harm, pain, and suffering."

A great illustration of this point is the story of Shadrach, Meshach, and Abednego.

> If we are thrown into the blazing furnace, the God we serve is able to save us from it, and he will rescue us from your hand, O king.
>
> But even if he does not, we want you to know, O king, that we will not serve your gods or worship the image of gold you have set up.
>
> Daniel 3:17–18 (NIV)

This is a great example of trust and hope. They trusted in the ability of God to save them from death, but at the same time all they could do was hope he would. They declared that even if God didn't save them their trust wouldn't be shaken.

Now you may say that you do not hope for those things but that you have faith that God will do those things. My question to you is what are we called to put our faith in? Our faith should be in God and only God, right? God will keep his promises, but it may not be and probably isn't the way we hoped it would be. Much of it depends on us and if we are going to listen to what he is telling us to do so that he can bless us the way that he wants to. Where do we get a picture of a truly trustworthy God?

> Therefore I tell you, do not worry about your life, what you will eat or drink; or about your body, what you will wear. Is not life more important than food, and the body more important than clothes?

Look at the birds of the air; they do not sow or reap or store away in barns, and yet your heavenly Father feeds them. Are you not much more valuable than they?

Who of you by worrying can add a single hour to his life?

And why do you worry about clothes? See how the lilies of the field grow. They do not labor or spin.

Yet I tell you that not even Solomon in all his splendor was dressed like one of these.

If that is how God clothes the grass of the field, which is here today and tomorrow is thrown into the fire, will he not much more clothe you, O you of little faith?

So do not worry, saying, "What shall we eat?" or "What shall we drink?" or "What shall we wear?"

For the pagans run after all these things, and your heavenly Father knows that you need them.

But seek first his kingdom and his righteousness, and all these things will be given to you as well.

Therefore do not worry about tomorrow, for tomorrow will worry about itself. Each day has enough trouble of its own.

Matthew 6:25–34 (NIV)

Know that God will provide all of your needs but it may not be and probably is not the way you think, and it may be very hard to submit to the way he wants to teach you. I trust in God and in his promises as I walk in obedience. The only reason I personally can do that is because of the healing he has brought me through. So when you say you are trusting in God, are you really? Or are you just hoping he will do for you what you want him to do? Trust is not what we thought it was even with God.

Everybody wants someone to trust in. This is a glaring need in our lives not just because we have seen and experienced betrayal but because most of us have no foundation of trust in our lives at all, even believers. We find we can't trust ourselves, our spouses aren't as trustworthy as we hoped, and our perception of God makes him unreliable. How can we hope to exist in meaningful relationships like this?

Expectation

So let's talk a little about expectation. Any therapist or marriage counselor that is worth being paid will tell you that you should not enter a marriage with unrealistic expectations. I submit to you that any expectations at all are unrealistic.

Expectations are either positive or negative. There does not seem to be a middle ground. Trust and expectation appear to be the same thing. If you cannot have expectations then you cannot have trust. If I expect something to happen, I am assured that it will happen. If I expect a table to not fall down when I put a plate of food on it, I trust it. If that table crumbles, I am upset and disappointed, and my level of trust in it declines, as well as my expectation that it will stand next time I place food on it. Now as the table proves itself worthy over the course of time, my trust will rise along with my expectation. I am not saying that this is right because we are not to put trust in anyone or thing that is not God or of God, but this is the way we operate.

Whether or not they are the same is debatable. What is not debatable is that most of us use expectation in the same context as we use trust. Someone told me that we should be able to enter a marriage relationship expecting that our spouses will stay loyal to us. So bear with me. Now we are entering marriage with expectations, which are wrong, right? Okay, then, say we should be able to enter a marriage relationship trusting that our spouses will stay loyal to us. Sorry. It just cannot happen. You cannot put your trust in your spouse. You just cannot. So then what? Do we immediately go in the opposite direction and expect that our spouses will break our trust and let us down in some way or multiple ways? No, we do not do that either.

These are called "bitter root expectations," by the way, and a man named Jack Frost does an excellent teaching on this and "bitter root judgments." Well, is there a neutral ground between positive expectations and bitter expectations that we are called to live at? Yes, there is, and you probably will not like it. It is called hope.

Hope

I am sorry to break this to you, but hope is the best we can get in relationships with people. If you want to expect something, expect that hope is the best you can do in your relationship with your spouse and everyone else. This is going to make most of you very uncomfortable because hope lives in a realm of uncertainty, and we do not want to live there in our relationships with the people that can hurt us the most. Well, you are going to have to come to grips with it.

We are devastated because we are trying to live in a place that is uninhabitable to us. We are trying to live in a place of trust, and that place does not exist except where God is. So we set up shop out in limbo, and when trust is shattered, we come crashing down and are down for a while. Then some of us try to live back in that limbo of imaginable trust again while some of us stay down and get bitter. We come to the conclusion that we cannot trust anyone, which is truth, but then we never open up to anyone emotionally again because we are afraid of getting hurt. Meanwhile, those of us who cannot live in a world where there is no trust in relationships are busy getting shattered and slammed again and again and again. Is either of these an attractive offer?

So then let's set ourselves up in hope. You're already there; just settle down. Is hope enough? How can you live in a marriage relationship just hoping that your spouse is not going to cheat on you or leave you? If the best that we can do in our marriage is hope that we will not get torn apart, what's the point of getting married? Why not just hope in friend relationships? At least when friends let you down or betray you, it is not as painful as it is with a spouse.

God is the only one we can place our trust in. Some have argued that we should still be able to trust in people, just not to the degree that we trust in God. I don't see biblical provision for that statement. I will mention again that what we see in the Bible is "trust in the Lord your God." The Bible does not say, "Trust in the Lord your God with the most trust, and then trust in your spouse a little less." The Bible does not talk about different levels of trust.

Now let's get into semantics and why it's not enough to just swap words without a real change in perspective. It's important to have a shift in perspective because if you just swap words, then "hope" is going to carry the same weight for you that "trust" carried for you. What I am talking about here is not a change in semantics but a change in perspective. That change in perspective is all about removing the "assurance" from your spouse and replacing it with uncertainty. Why the heck would we want to do that, and why the heck would I think that God wants us to do that? Because assurance equals security, and we are not to find security in anything except God. Our assurance needs to be in God and God alone, and when we put it in other things, we are just asking for it to be shaken. God will not allow us to live in perfect peace if our assurance and security are found in other things. He will allow our worlds and everything that we have security in to be shaken and rattled. Many of you have experienced this in jobs, family, marriages, and finances. I know that I have. Oh, have I ever.

> You will keep him in perfect peace him whose mind is steadfast, because he trusts in you.
>
> Isaiah 26:3 (NIV)

Don't worry and don't get discouraged. There is a point and hope is enough. Keep reading.

Loyalty

We are all looking for someone to be loyal to us. It is a natural thing; God created the passion to know and experience loyalty inside of us.

What makes a loyal person? Is it someone to fight our battles with us, both emotional and even physical? Is it someone to gossip with? Is it someone who will not go, after gossiping with us, and gossip about us to someone else? Is it someone to hold our hair back when we are puking our guts out? Is it someone that will not betray us? Is it someone who will spot us five bucks for lunch when we are short? Is it someone who just listens when we are hurting and buys us comfort food? Someone who will never leave us?

I will use a relationship for this example that is very close to me. He has been my best friend for twenty or so years. Since sixth grade we have been like brothers. He is someone I would say is loyal. He has left me alone during physical fights and emotional battles. He has refused to gossip with me and has talked about me to other people. He has never held my hair back while I was vomiting. He has betrayed my trust. He has not had any money to give me even if I was short on lunch money. He has not had time to listen to me when I am hurting and has not bought me any comfort food. He has left me and moved away. Now he sounds like a crappy friend. Even as I am writing this, I am asking myself, "Are you sure you are best friends with this jerk?"

Does the fact that he has done or not done all of these things that demonstrate loyalty make him a terrible friend? Absolutely not! You think you know someone who can hold all of these characteristics all of the time? Impossible! There is no one on this earth who can be all of these things all of the time. Oh wait, I step on that person every time I walk into my house. It is called a doormat. There are people that try, but eventually they fail to be something for someone. The result is a shame-and-guilt spiral, and the only way out is to try to be even more for more people. So if that is you, knock it off, will you? I do believe that at different times we can take on a couple of the characteristics of loyalty successfully, but to own the title of "loyal" is impossible for anyone on this earth.

The major item that comes to mind when loyalty is discussed is the topic of staying faithful to our spouses. But what else does loyalty look like in our marriage relationships?

Have you ever found out your spouse had been complaining and talking negatively about you to other people? How did that make you feel? How many times have you criticized your spouse in front of someone else? How do you think that made your spouse feel? When it happens, does it feel like a breach in loyalty to you? A loyal person does not gossip about us to other people, right? Yet we find that many times the quickest road to a physical affair is when an emotional affair is formed. Many times an emotional affair is born out of the critical gossip about a person's spouse with a person outside of the marriage.

Gossip is running rampant in our marriages. Think about getting together with a group of friends. Let's make it ladies' night out or men's night out. Has the conversation ever turned toward complaining about your spouses? If it did, how ready and eager were you to offer your own two cents into the pot? If most of us would be honest, we would probably say "pretty ready and eager." How loyal is that?

Many people attach loyalty to the willingness of their spouses to listen to them talk. I can think of many times over the years my wife has called me at work. She has been home with the kids all day long and just wants to talk to an adult. What better adult to talk to than the person who is supposed to be your best friend? So she would call me, and so many times I hurried her off the phone because I was busy with something else. It didn't matter what the reason was that I rushed her off the phone. The message she received was always the same—"You're not important enough for me to give you my attention."

In her mind I was supposed to be the one who would make time for her no matter what because that's what husbands do for their wives and vice versa. That is what a loyal husband or wife is, right? They will always make time to listen to whatever it is we want to say. Loyal husbands and wives will listen to what we think is important and agree with us. I remember a couple of different times I came to my wife with something that was exciting to me only to hear a negative remark about it. It was such a let-down because I wanted her to stand beside me and she didn't. I wanted to feel that loyalty and I didn't.

Does your spouse always fight battles with you, or do you feel like you are on your own? Is your spouse ready to come beside you when you have been the victim of injustice? We hope so, right? Is it always a reality? No. My wife used to work at a bank as a teller. She had a boss who was not the nicest person in the world. Many times my wife would come home and complain about this boss. I had done my best to listen each time and offer any encouragement I could. One night my wife came home and started telling me all about what her boss did that particular day. I looked at my wife and said, "Unless you are going to do something about this situation, I don't want to hear about it anymore." How do you think that affected my wife? It was devastating for her because I had made it unsafe for her to talk to me about anything involving work. She was struggling with a situation, and I essentially abandoned her. I became someone who was not going to fight her battle with her.

Do you feel that your spouse is ready to fight all of your battles with you? I have encountered many in ministry who would answer no. This could get very real for many of you with this question: Do you feel your spouse would stand by your side in a conflict involving you and his/her parents?

Many of us have different views and ideas of what it means to be loyal. However, when we enter marriage expecting our spouses to meet our standards of loyalty all of the time, we are going to live in disappointment. Nobody can wear the title of "loyal" because sooner or later we will all fail to meet the standard of loyalty no matter what it looks like.

So we come back to the conclusion that God has placed the passion to feel and experience loyalty in us. However, this God-given passion has been warped by the enemy and turned into an ungodly thing in us. The purpose was not that we look to other people for loyalty but that we look to our God and Lord Jesus Christ to be loyalty for us.

> Be strong and of a good courage, fear not, nor be afraid of them: for the LORD thy God, he it is that doth go with thee; he will not fail thee, nor forsake thee.
>
> Deuteronomy 31:6

This is a favorite verse of mine. There are many verses in the Bible about how God will never fail us or forsake us. Isn't that real loyalty? There are fifty-eight verses in the Bible that talk about how God will never forsake us. God is the only one that we can trust to be 100 percent loyal to us. He will always listen to us, fight our battles with us, and will never betray us. I did not say that he will be loyal to what we want all the time, but he will be loyal to everything that we need as long as we are walking with him.

So if we cannot even trust that our spouses will be loyal, then what's the point of entering into relationship with them?

Someone to Depend On

What does it mean if someone is dependable? What does it mean if your spouse is dependable? A dependable person would be someone that can be trusted to complete tasks. A dependable person is someone that keeps promises. A dependable person will remember to do things the way that you like them to be done. A dependable person will not let us down. We can lean on those people. We can trust that they will lift us up when we are down.

As I think back on the ways I thought a dependable wife should be, here are some of the conclusions that I came up with. A dependable wife will clean the house once a week. A dependable wife will help out with typical man chores, like mowing the lawn and taking out the trash, when I am busy with work. A dependable wife will take care of the children by feeding them and bathing them. A dependable wife will not lose things. She will put the vehicle keys back in the basket so that they do not get lost. She will not lie or spend money frivolously. She will cook dinner. She will stay faithful. She will send birthday cards out to the extended family on their birthdays and do all the Christmas and birthday shopping. She will also do the grocery shopping. A dependable wife will be intimate when I want to be intimate. Men, you may have some other ideas of what a dependable wife is and should be.

Women, you probably have some different ideas of what makes a dependable husband. You may say a dependable husband will help with chores around the house and pick up after himself. He will do the man chores like mowing the lawn and taking out the trash. He will take care of the bills that need to be paid. He will provide for the family by whatever means necessary even if it means getting two or three jobs. He will make it possible for you to stay at home with the kids and not have to work. He will help out with the kids and do things with them like take them to the park and do other things that you have decided makes a good father. He will discipline the children so you do not have to. He will ask you how you are doing and be able to know when something is wrong with you even if you do not tell him. He will be the spiritual leader of the house. He will listen to you when you talk. He will share his feelings. He will not look at other women. He will stay faithful to you. There may be other things that you could list here that I am leaving out.

I know that if my wife expects me to be all of these things all of the time we are in big trouble. I know that if I expect my wife to be all of these things at the same time then we are in big trouble. At different times we can take on some of these characteristics and maybe all of them at different points of time. However, we cannot be all of them all the time. We will never measure up to the things we view makes us dependable people all of the time.

I have failed at all of these things many times over the years. I have also succeeded in being that person for my wife at different times. We have a tendency to look and focus on the negative. If you ask your spouse to list the times that you have proven to not be dependable and then list the times you have been, I am sure the times you have not been would be the much longer list and come much quicker. Does that mean we are constantly walking around with our spouses viewing them as not dependable and just waiting for them to let us down again? How many times have you said to yourself or complained to someone else, "He or she is just not there for me"? Do you feel like your spouse is married to the gym or married to the job? How about married to a favorite sports team? Do you feel like your spouse would be more dependable for these other things?

What about promises? As I reflect, there have been many times that my son has wanted me to come upstairs or outside to do something with him. I have told him that I would be "right there." Well, things happen and I get distracted, and it takes me awhile to get there. What do you think that does to my son's perception of "I will be right there"? Do you think that he will depend on me to be right there when I say I will be? How about when you tell your spouse that you promise you will be home from work at a certain time? Well, things happen, and you do not make it. Your spouse had dinner ready at the time you said you were going to be home, and you were not. That has been the case for me a handful of times. So that is a broken promise, and you have made your spouse feel unappreciated because he/she had dinner ready for you.

What about other broken promises? "I promise I will stop drinking." "I promise I will stop gambling." "I promise I will never look at pornography again." Even "I promise I will stop spending money or using the credit card." I'm sure we could spend a lot of time listing all of the promises we have heard from our spouses. Every time it happens again, it is a broken promise, and you realize a little more each time that you cannot depend on this person to do what he or she says. But we push that feeling down because you have to be able to depend on your spouse, right? I mean, to not depend on your spouse would just be crazy.

Eventually we all prove ourselves not to be dependable. And every time we fail, a little bitterness and resentment is created in our spouse because the expectation failed. So if we cannot even depend on our spouses, what's the point of getting married?

?

Sharing Our Lives
and Intimacy

We want someone to share our life with. We all have the desire to find someone special that we can share our life with. We want someone to be able to talk to when we are excited and to brag to when something great happens to us. We really want to do those things with someone that we know cares about us and gets excited with us.

Okay, so what happens when you are single and have no one to tell good things to that would get excited with you? Let's say you are golfing and hit a hole in one but you are by yourself and have no one around to tell. I have a personal example. I didn't hit a hole in one, but I did catch the biggest bass I have ever caught. It was a personal best, and guess what: I was all by myself. I was actually at a private lake that I was technically not supposed to be at. When I caught that fish, I was yelling at the security guards just because I wanted to show someone. Well, not even the security guards heard me, so nobody saw this fish except me. I started to feel bad. I started to feel a little depressed and very alone. I immediately wished that I was not the only one out there fishing and that I could have interaction with someone even if it was the security guard.

Now take those same feelings and put them into everyday life. If there was a time in your life when you were all by yourself, you experienced that feeling often. It probably was not even the exciting times that you wanted to be able to share with someone that would care but everyday life things. The things that hurt you and the things brought you down. Watching a television show that you like with someone who likes it as well. Someone to eat with and joke with.

We want to be in communion with others. Even the people who say that they do not need or want anybody else actually do need and want others. They have just been so hurt by people that they do not see how it is possible to be in relationship with people and not get hurt. But they do want that if it is possible.

Why do we want someone to share our lives with? The answer to that question is that we are afraid of being alone. I think many of us know that place, and we will do anything to keep from going back there. What's the best way to make sure you will always have someone with you to share and be with? Let's get married! For some of you the fear of being alone is so great and overwhelming that this is the only reason you decided to get married.

There is depression in being alone. Two things that are usually stated together are "alone and depressed." The fear of being alone has made its way into songs. Artist Al Green wrote a song about being alone. A part of it says: "I am so tired of being alone. I am so tired of on-my-own. Won't you help me, girl, just as soon as you can?" It is the substance of musical lyrics. Nobody wants to be alone. It is not a fun place to be.

One person said, "I think I fear being alone more than I fear death. I know it's really strange, but I equate loneliness with not being loved, which I know is not true but that's the picture I have in my mind." I took this quote from a Web site that allows people who are alone or feel alone to post comments and post their stories. Many of us fear being alone more than we fear death. So being married takes care of that fear, right? Now that we are married, we do not need to feel alone, right?

I wish that was the truth. I wish that we could get married and rely on our spouses to provide the companionship that we long for.

Is it possible that we can be married and still be lonely? Absolutely, it is. Let me ask you a question. Are you someone that you would classify as "needy"? My wife was. I do not believe she is like that anymore. Maybe I should say that she is not "needy" for the same reasons that she used to be. She has also directed her "neediness" to the only one that can fulfill that for her.

A "needy" person always wants to be around people. "Needy" people hate to be alone. A lot of us just do not like being alone for extended periods of time, but "needy" people hate being alone for any length of time. Well, guess what. Your spouse cannot be around you twenty-four hours a day seven days a week. It just cannot happen. There is work. That accounts for the most time apart. This is not limited to only the needy people, but they are the ones who are affected before the rest.

But let's say that your spouse is a firefighter. So your spouse is gone for twenty-four hours at a time. Are you going to be okay with that? Are you going to be lonely? Let's say your spouse travels for his/her job. He or she is gone for weeks at a time. Are you going to be okay with that? Are you going to be lonely? Then let's add the fact that your spouse probably has hobbies and things he or she likes to do in his or her spare time. These hobbies may or may not include you. Fishing, for example, is very often an activity or hobby that the husband enjoys but the wife does not. So now you have a spouse that goes away for a week on business and then when he/she gets back goes fishing or does some other activity that does not include you. Or for most of us we go to work for eight hours through the day, and then when we get home and on the weekends, we spend time in our hobbies that may not include our spouse.

Also, what if your spouse does not open up to you emotionally? So you do not feel like you connect intimately. So now to you it does not seem that you and your spouse are spending any time together, and you feel alone and also rejected. You do not think your spouse even wants to spend time with you. We are devastated that we can be lonely in a marriage because we never saw that as a possibility.

So now what do we do? We are the very thing that we got married trying to avoid—lonely! So we try to find fulfillment in other things. We start going out with our friends more. If we are with friends, we cannot be lonely, right? But our friends cannot be with us all of the time. They have their own lives as well. They are busy with other things. So what do we turn to? Drugs? Alcohol? Maybe if we do some of these things we will not feel so lonely. Affairs? If another person looks at me and desires me, maybe we can have a connection and I will not be lonely. You are left wondering, *How in the world did I get here?* Many of us feel lonely in our marriages. I know my wife was lonely. God has healed that in her. Praise God for that. I would even be brave enough to say that most of us feel lonely in our marriages.

I read an article on CNN.com about married couples sleeping in separate beds. *Twenty-three percent* of married couples sleep alone. Do you think they get lonely sleeping by themselves when the one they love the most is just down the hall? Do you think that causes some separation between them? There were some comments by some people in that article that said sleeping alone has been great for their marriage. I do not buy that for one second.

Having said that, I do want to be sensitive to those of you who have been or are being tormented by the snoring of your spouses. Every third night I sleep in a room with three other firemen, so I completely understand how tormenting it is to try to sleep when someone is snoring up a storm. I understand how you could reach the conclusion that separate beds or rooms would be good for your marriages. I completely understand why you might feel justified by that decision. Then, of course, we have the people, such as my wife, who seem to think the whole bed is their conquered territory and claim it all night long. Many nights I have fallen asleep taking up half of the bed only to wake up crammed into a quarter of it. I wake up wondering, *How in the world did this happen?* I can understand the pull of potential space freedom separate beds would have.

Whatever the reason might be, whether the reasons I have mentioned or something else like "My spouse always eats sandwiches in bed and drops crumbs on my head," I can understand the rationalization and justification for separate beds and even rooms. My question is, does the fact you have rationalized and justified your decision make it right?

The ability to truly be intimate is what godly relationships are born from. It doesn't matter if the relationship is with God or our spouses; if we are not willing to be completely 100 percent intimate, then we do not have the ability to obtain godly relationships. The reason is because it's only through our willingness to be intimate at all costs that we can receive understanding and revelation of the perfect love of God. Without intimacy there is no understanding of love.

Satan, our enemy, will do anything and everything he can in order to destroy intimacy because he knows if he can destroy intimacy he can defeat love in our lives. There is something so deeply intimate about sharing a bed with our spouses. I don't even understand it to be honest. There is a joining of our spirits together as we rest in the shadow of our Father's wings. Think about it. As we sleep we are side by side for an average of eight hours. When during the day can we have that much time together? Most of us spend our days apart because of work, chores, kid activities, etc. If we lose that time together at night, eight hours of intimacy are gone. We will begin to feel the consequences of this eventually as our feelings of intimacy begin to erode. Unexplainable loneliness and sadness will begin to creep into our souls. We will begin to resent our spouses and can't even explain why. The feelings of separation will grow, and before long we will be saying, "We never spend any time together anymore."

My advice is to stop viewing snoring, space domination, etc., as problems that cannot be resolved and start viewing them as an attack from Satan on the intimacy of marriage relationships. Bind the attacks in the name of Jesus. Pray against them. Get snoring machines or bigger beds. Use a plate so that the crumbs don't fall on your wife's or husband's head.

If being separated from each other is great for your marriage, there is a problem that needs to be addressed. A good friend of mine that worked for the fire department years ago told me one time that if his schedule was not on for twenty-four hours and off for forty-eight his marriage would not survive. He said it survives because he goes away every third day. There is something very wrong with that statement. I have found that going away for twenty-four hours actually hurts my relationship with my wife at times but never makes it better.

I would say to the married couples who are sleeping alone, "What else are you doing alone?" That is a slippery slope. Here are some real comments from real people taken from Yahoo.com:

> funny thing, I spent the loneliest of years when I was married (25 yrs) then, when I was single, it was okay to be alone—I enjoyed it. now in the relationship i'm in, I am lonely again. I guess it's because we have an expectation of someone "sharing our lives" and when it's not that way or the person you live with doesn't wish to talk or listen, you feel lonely! so I TRY to find interests of my own and not depend on my partner for company.

So this person got married to have someone to share her life with. That was one of her reasons anyway. She understands the hard way that she cannot depend on her partner to keep her from being lonely. So my question is and you have to ask yourself, did you get married to have someone to share your life with, or did you get married because you did not want to be lonely? Here is another testimony:

> I've been married for five years, and for the past two I have been feeling alone. We have two beautiful kids. My husband is a commercial fisherman. In his world, this is the order of things: The kids come first, then fishing and then our marriage. He says it's because we have no time and no money. He likes to say, "Wait until mackerel season is finished and then we'll start working on us." But mackerel season came and went. It was a bad season, so now I have to wait for another good season. I wish he could see me as a woman who needs to feel special, not just as a working mother of two and a housemaid. How do I do this?

Priorities play a big role in this. Unfortunately, we have our priorities all messed up. This is important because if we get married looking to eliminate loneliness, we expect to be the highest priority our spouses have next to God. This expectation is undermined when children, work, friends, or even hobbies come before our marriage relationships. The undermining of this expectation breeds resentment and bitterness. This may sound exactly like what many of you are going through or the way you have been feeling. We can plug in different things our spouses put before us, but the theme is the same. Do you want a good example of how many people are lonely in their marriages? Type in Google "lonely marriage" and see how many links there are to Web sites that will help you have an affair with other married people. It is very sad. People are making money off the loneliness that exists in marriage. There are millions of married women signed up for these sites looking to get matched with a partner for an affair. Some of these sites have little taglines for the women pictured where they can tell a little about themselves. The phrase "I am lonely" is in almost every one of them.

Many people are using the Internet to ease their loneliness. According to Divorce Magazine, only 46 percent of married men believe that an online affair is adultery. Seventy-five percent of married people believe that it is okay to visit an adult site on the Internet. Other sources indicate that:

- 57 percent of people have used the Internet to flirt.
- 38 percent of people have engaged in explicit online sexual conversation.
- 50 percent of people have talked on the phone with someone they first chatted with online.
- 31 percent of people have had an online conversation that has led to in-person sex.

I want to take a little time here to talk to you about a specific scripture in the Bible that I believe has been very misinterpreted and misunderstood. It is this:

> And the LORD God said, It is not good that the man should be alone; I will make him an help meet for him.
>
> Genesis 2:18

What have we been taught that this verse says? We have been taught that God said it is not good for man to be alone and so that is why he created woman so that we would not be alone and therefore not be lonely. In Genesis 2:20 it talks about the woman being of Adam's flesh, and then we get the famous verse:

> Therefore shall a man leave his father and his mother, and shall cleave unto his wife: and they shall be one flesh.
>
> Genesis 2:24

I believe we have made a mistake in how we have interpreted these two passages. Let us look first at the fact that the verse immediately following verse eighteen talks about God creating the animals and bringing them before Adam to name them. The point that I am making is to ask yourself, "What, if anything, is God saying about marriage in verse eighteen?" The answer that I am submitting is that God is not saying anything about the intimate covenant of marriage in verse eighteen and that it is much simpler than we have made it.

God says that it is not good for man to be alone so he made him a "help meet." The original Hebrew word means for help means *aid,* and the original Hebrew word for meet means *counterpart.* So if you break it down realizing that in different languages the adjective that describes the noun comes after the noun, it would read that God made an *aid* for us that is a *counterpart.* The NIV says, "I will make him a helper suitable for him." If verse eighteen is talking about marriage, then I doubt that Paul would have had anything negative to say about marriage at all. But Paul says in 1 Corinthians that it is good not to marry because when we marry we care about the concerns of our spouses. Paul basically refers to marriage as a distraction. Now we also know that that is just Paul's opinion. However, if when God says that it is not good for man to be alone and we interpret the second part of that verse to mean that is why God created marriage, I do not think Paul would have said that it is good not to marry. Well, we can have helpers outside of a marriage relationship, can we not? I interact with lots of women throughout the day who help me with things, and I am not, nor do I want to be, in marriage covenant with them. One wife is enough.

There is another misunderstanding that we need to examine regarding the interpretation of this verse. I am submitting to you that it was never God's design to create other people so that we would not be lonely. I was listening to a teaching taught by a much-respected man. This man is in a key position of leadership in a well-known international ministry. I enjoy listening to his teachings. However, he was talking about the Genesis 2:18 verse in this teaching, and he said something that I think most of us were brought up to believe. He was talking about Adam in the garden. He said that Adam was walking in the garden and started to feel something he had never felt before. He started to have a longing in his spirit that he was not familiar with. Adam was lonely. Now I am driving in my car while I am listening to this, and I turn to the CD player and shout, "No!" I feel that God had given me revelation into this verse the night before I heard this teaching, so it was still very fresh in my head.

Let me paint you a picture. Here is Adam. He is in paradise. He is in a world where there is no sin. There is nothing ungodly about this place yet. Adam had a one-on-one close, intimate relationship with our Lord and God. God walked through this garden. God spoke audibly to Adam. They had the kind of relationship that we all long to have with God. This is the closest picture that we have of a paradise with God. It is, in my opinion, what heaven and eternity with my Jesus is going to be like.

Where do we get the audacity to claim that Adam was lonely in this place? This is like a slap in the face to God. To say that this kind of relationship and environment was not enough and that we needed God to create woman so that we would not be lonely is just ridiculous. If that is true, what do we have to look forward to? If that were true, then we would be looking at an eternity where it is possible to become bored with the arrangement and then to become lonely. Let's also take into consideration that without sin it is impossible to be lonely. Being lonely is rooted in sin. Loneliness comes from ungodly things, for example: the fear of abandonment, fear of being alone, self-hatred, rejection, bitterness, and unforgiveness to name a few. Well, there was no sin in the garden at that time, so there was no loneliness. There is no biblical reference to be able to assume that loneliness is what Adam was feeling.

So God said, "It is not good that man be alone." He never

says, nor can you imply, that he created woman so the man would not be lonely. He says that woman was created to be a helper, or aid. Adam experienced more fulfillment in his relationship with God than we could ever imagine. So why did God say that it is not good for man to be alone? The answer is very simple. Which one of you out there can accomplish everything by yourself? Some of you think you can, but really we all need people to help us, right? God knew that we need other people to help us along the way. It is not good for man to be alone because there is just too much to do for just one person to get done. Did you ever stop to think about how long it must have taken Adam to name all the animals? Also, last time I checked, men cannot give birth. Unless it was different in the beginning, we need help procreating. We need helpers, but the only answer for loneliness is an intimate relationship with God.

By the way, if you are thinking that your children will provide you with what you need so you will not be lonely, you are sadly mistaken. If you are counting on that interaction to give you purpose and fulfillment, then you need to realize that your kids cannot be with you twenty-four-seven either, and eventually they will leave home and you will be in the same position. So, people, here is the conclusion. If we cannot be protected from being alone and feeling lonely, then what's the point of getting married?

Someone to Share Intimacy

We desire to have someone to be intimate with, don't we? Not just sexually but emotionally. To be deeply intimate; to be laid bare before each other! Most women greatly desire this, or at least that is what we are told by society. But men have just as great of a need for real intimacy as women do. We were all created with the need for intimacy. As much as we men do not want to admit it, we need it.

So what is intimacy? Webster defines intimacy as:

The state of being intimate; familiarity

I asked a couple of people for their idea of intimacy, and here are some of the responses:

"I think intimacy is different for every person."

"Intimacy is knowing and doing what the other person wants without them having to ask you or tell you."

"Intimacy is being unguarded and openly honest. It is allowing the other person to see the real you. Adam and Eve naked in the garden and not being ashamed, that is intimacy."

Intimacy in a marriage relationship is being completely laid bare before your spouse. It is the ability to "be" with your spouse just as you are. It is the ability to share your hopes and fears and every emotion that you have at any time. Being able to just lay there with your spouse in bed and not even have to say anything but just being together. Not just showing superficial emotion; for example, when you smash your finger with a hammer, you show the anger emotion. That is a superficial emotion. Intimate emotions I would classify as emotions that come from who you really are. So let's explore what an intimate emotion might be.

Let's use an example of a hypothetical conflict. My wife comes to me and says that she is going out with her friends on a night that we were supposed to spend together. So she does, and I am upset. She comes back home, and I tell her that she hurt me. I tell her that she hurt me because we were supposed to spend the night together and I was looking forward to it. She apologizes, and we kiss and make up with a plan to spend the next night together. This is good, right? This is how we have been taught to deal with hurt and pain. Heck, most of us do not even do this. Most of us who can make it to that point give ourselves a pat on the back for being such good communicators and addressing problems as they arise.

However, is this enough, or is there a much deeper level of emotion that you are protecting by stopping at "you hurt me"? What about addressing the reason why it hurt you? We did that by saying that we were looking forward to spending time with them, right? What about addressing the real reason that it hurt you and why it hurt so badly? Why don't you address the fact that deep down you have judged that you are a bad husband/wife, a bad person, unattractive, and that you are lucky to have your spouse? What you are really hearing when your spouse says that he/she wants to spend some time with someone else is that you are a bad husband/wife, ugly, not fun to be around, a bad person, and that he/she might want to leave you for someone better. So your spouse has just reinforced what you already believe about yourself, and we hear rejection and feel the weight of rejection. The emotions that come from your inner being that are directly related to what your impression of yourself is are intimate emotions. That is intimacy.

So how many of us even really want that kind of intimacy? You may say, "Of course I do," on the outside as an immediate response, but if you really get honest with yourself, you may come up with a different answer. Attaining this type of intimacy comes at a price. You have to lay yourself bare. You have to put all of your insecurities on the line and hope that you are not going to be rejected because of it. You have to put all of your fears out there. You have to be willing to lay bare all of your imperfections and inabilities to be the person that you feel you should be for your spouse. There is actually real risk here.

I am not going to blow smoke at you in this. If you do all of this, there is a chance that your spouse will reject it because of his or her unwillingness to do the same thing. Let me tell you why I think we have such a hard time with this. It is because we do not like ourselves very much at all. It is because we do not feel like we measure up to our spouse's expectations. It is because we fear rejection. It is because we do not feel adequate. It is because if our spouses knew who we really are, they would lose all confidence in us. Let me ask you again. Do you really want that kind of intimacy?

I was in emotional lockdown for eight years. During the first four years of my marriage, I could not access emotions. The reasons for this went way back for me and were woven into the pain of rejection and perceived abandonment. I knew there was something wrong with me, but I didn't know how to fix it. Emotional walls block our ability to be intimate with anyone, let alone our spouses. I was unable to connect intimately with my wife because I didn't know how to feel. The result was much loneliness, irritability, and anger. In an amazing season of my life, God broke the emotional bondage I had allowed to take over my life. As I was healed from that bondage, I began to feel, and it was amazing. I also began to open up to my wife and to lay myself bare before her. It was not all right away, but it was and has been a process. Well, I began to realize that I had been so wrapped up in my own emotional bondage that I never realized my wife was wrapped up in the same bondage. Not quite to my extreme, but I began to realize that she had never truly opened herself and laid herself bare to me. I realized that I did not know my wife intimately. She had never let me in to who she really was and is.

Women are not more intimate than men because of the simple fact that when you hate yourself you are not going to let anyone in to see who you really are. You are going to put up a front so people cannot see the real you, and that includes your spouse. Women hate themselves just as much as men hate themselves. There is not a gender that is less vulnerable to self-hate than the other. Let me take it even a step further and say that when you have lived in self-hate for so long, you do not even know how to let someone in to your real self. Unfortunately, I have never seen anyone, with the exception of those that have been through ministry addressing the spirits of the unloving—which are self-unforgiveness, self-bitterness, rejection, resentment, anger, violence, wrath, hatred, and self-murder—really love and accept themselves. Also the fear of abandonment and not measuring up are part of the unloving bondage. If you have not walked through healing for these, there is an excellent chance that you are in bondage to the unloving in varying degrees.

The scheme gets woven into us when we are young, and society helps engrave it. Also, the "bad" things that we do throughout our lives that we never forgive ourselves for entrench these spirits. Women get credit for being more intimate because they are more *emotional* than men most of the time. There is a big difference between being intimate and being emotional. I hate to use my wife again as an example, but I think that she was much more emotional than I was. She displayed a much wider range of emotions than I did, but they were always superficial emotions. There was nothing of great depth that she would share. There was nothing intimate. It is the same for a lot of women. Men, you may have never even thought about it, but think about it now and ask yourself these questions: Do you really know your wife? Do you know her heart? Do you know how she really feels about herself, you, and everything? My point is that women have not cornered the market on intimacy.

* * *

From Kara:

I was an incredibly needy person. As a child and teenager, I remember my parents going out on a date and feeling very down until they were home. When I married Jesse, I wanted him to go everywhere with me: the grocery store, the gas station, the mall, the bank, even the bathroom. Anywhere I went, I wanted him there. Yes, it was partly because I loved him and enjoyed spending time with him, but it also had a great deal to do with the fact I did not want to be alone. I absolutely equated being alone to being lonely. There was no difference for me between the two words.

Poor Jesse—if he would get up from the couch, I would ask him where he was going. His reply would be, "To the bathroom, is that okay?" It was that bad! I now see that there is a difference between being alone and being lonely. Jesse works twenty-four-hour shifts at the fire station, I am without a doubt *alone* during most of this time (at least without adult interaction), but I am no longer *lonely*. Do I miss him? Like crazy, but when you are aware of God's constant presence, how can you be lonely?

Now about this intimacy business, I was convinced that I was an expert at being intimate with Jesse but that he was unable to open up to me. Again, it wasn't until recently that Jesse and I realized that I was never truly intimate with him. Sure, I would tell him if I was sad, or mad, or happy, but that was about the extent of it. I thought I had it down because Jesse would hardly share these things with me. I never told him the deep and intimate feelings behind those emotions. I also believed myself to be an intimacy professional because I loved to snuggle and be touched. I now recognize those needs, at the time, as my way of feeling validated by Jesse. Do I love to snuggle and be touched by Jesse now? More than ever because now I am aware of the deep love and intimacy behind these touches.

* * *

So if having someone to be intimate with no longer seems like a viable option and you have realized that a lot of us do not even really want that or feel comfortable with that, what's the point of getting married?

?

Make Me Feel Good!

Here is an interesting reason why some of us get married. We tend to think that the person we marry is always going to make us feel good about ourselves.

Men, we think our wives are going to be constantly telling us how good looking we are, right? How we are such great providers. How we are the best fathers and husbands in the world. How we are the great protectors of the family. Our wives are going to show us the respect that we deserve and need, right? Of course they will recognize that when we are home after working all day long we need to relax and not be bothered with any household chores, and they will pamper us and make us feel great.

Women, you think that your husbands are always going to tell you how beautiful you are. We will tell you how great of a job you do around the house in keeping it clean and what a great mother you are. We will always make you feel so appreciated, right? We will always tell you what a great wife you are.

We will always notice when you change your hair color or get a haircut and tell you how beautiful you look. We will be intuitive and know what to compliment you on and when to do it. We men will show you how much we appreciate and love you by showering you with gifts and cards. We will also help you with chores around the house and with the kids because we will understand that job is not so easy. We will snuggle with you all the time and never look at any other women. We will certainly never look at pornography.

Even though most of us know that this is not reality, there is something in us that holds on to most of these expectations, and we are constantly let down. Unfortunately, when we are let down in these areas, we do not feel very good about ourselves. I believe the following principle to be true: if you hate yourself before you get married, you are going to hate yourself after you get married. Unfortunately, most of us hate ourselves before we get married.

How long have you been married? What I am about to say relates to people who have been married for fifty years or one year. As you think over the years you have been married, whether they are few or many, has your spouse ever been able to change your perception about who you are as a person?

I know that there are many times our spouses make us feel good and bad throughout the course of a day. When we feel good or bad, depending on how our spouses interact with us, we are displaying an emotional response. There is a difference between an emotional response and who you believe you are as a person. The emotional response is self-esteem, and there is a line between self-esteem and what you really believe or know to be true about yourself. If you do not believe me, walk by a mirror and see what thoughts come to mind. I am willing to bet that you think the same about yourself when you look in the mirror today as you did when you looked in the mirror before you got married. Actually, many of you probably feel worse about yourself today than you did back then.

It does not matter if our spouses say something during the day to make us feel good about ourselves emotionally because when we stand in front of that mirror what we really believe comes to the surface. We may have changed some things on the outside, but when we look in the mirror, we are forced to see who we really are and what we really think about ourselves. I encourage you to try to find someone who can honestly tell you when he/she looks in the mirror he/she says, "I am so beautiful." Go find someone whose first thoughts when they walk by a mirror are not negative. When you find this person, let me know because I want to be the first one to call them a liar. I know from experience that even when you walk through healing for the unloving there are times that you still get attacked when you look in the mirror.

I did not like myself very much before I got married. Today I love what God loves and praise God for that healing, but there was nothing over the years that my wife told me that changed my belief of who I was. It was not that she never complimented me because she did a lot. I was not receiving it because I was in bondage.

Wives, do your husbands ever tell you how beautiful you are? Do they tell you that you are godly women and great wives? Do they tell you that you are the best mother in the world? Do they tell you that you are the greatest blessing they have ever received? Husbands, do your wives ever tell you how good looking they think you are? Do they tell you that you are a great provider and that they don't worry about things because they know you will provide? Do they tell you that you are great husbands and great fathers? Do they tell you that there is no other man for them? Do they assure you that you are not a failure? The first question is "Do we even hear our spouse when they give us compliments?" and the second question is "If you do hear them, does the feeling of validation last for more than five minutes?"

My wife also walked through healing for the unloving. I remember giving her compliments, and I knew they were not being received. A good way to gauge whether or not your compliments are being received is if your spouses are spitting compliments back at you right away. When they do this they are usually deflecting because they do not feel that they are worthy of the compliment. There are other more obvious ways we know that a compliment is not received. We say things like "yeah right" and "whatever." I did not know how to tell her things so that she would receive them. I know now that there is nothing I can do or could have done to make her receive those things in her spirit. That takes God and only God.

How about this: Does your spouse ever say anything negative about you? This can be in front of you or behind your back. It has become socially acceptable to give each other a hard time and to tease each other. I know that most of the time we do this it is done in a joking, light way. We are usually laughing when we tease each other. The problem is when a person is in bondage to the unloving those negative things hit and stick. When things are said in front of other people, they hit extra hard. Even though we are joking, we are thinking, *Not only does my spouse think this, but now it is out there for these other people to see.*

Does this mean that we should not tease each other? That would be hard for me and my wife because it is fun to go back and forth sometimes with playful banter. I guess the question you have to ask is "Is this building up or tearing down?" There is, obviously, a difference when things are said in anger and when things are said lightly, but I would ask you: how long do negative comments stick with you no matter what the motivation or circumstance is? Words have power and they stick to us. Unfortunately, negative words stick to us much longer than positive words.

Remember when I said that normally the good feeling from a compliment lasts only an hour or so before you forget it? Well, negative words stay with you for days. That is because it is just piling on to what you already believe about yourself. We have the remarkable ability to zero in on a person's greatest insecurities. So when we are teased by our spouses, we are almost always getting hit on something we already hate about ourselves. The pain and sting stay with us and only further solidify that self-hatred. So should we tease each other?

My wife and I try really hard not to tease each other with sarcasm and cutting remarks anymore. We feel that is what God wants for us. You and your spouses are going to have ask God what he wants for your marriage relationships. The point is that even in a marriage relationship we are still going to hear plenty of negative things said about us. No matter what context it is said in, it still hurts more coming from our spouses.

Next we move out of the realm of sarcasm, jokes, and teasing into the words we say out of anger. These are very damaging because our intention is to hurt and tear down. Our intention is to inflict emotional damage. We may be able to forgive our spouses when they attack us in this way, but we don't always see the deeper damage that is done as a result. It is a deeper wound that does not get healed because it hits on what you believe about yourself. It reinforces your beliefs.

How about the negative feelings you get not from what is said but what is not said? Women, you especially know what I am talking about. You are saying to yourself that you are the most important thing to your husband, so he should know everything about you and know instantly when something changes. Women, how does it make you feel when you get a new haircut or your hair cut at all and your husband does not say anything and does not even notice? Do you feel loved and special? Do you feel like you are your husband's world? Do you feel that he loves and cares about you? Do you feel validated? Do you feel beautiful? No! You feel little and insignificant. You do not feel that he pays attention to you and that you are not worthy of his time. The problem is that many men do not pay attention to those things, so this is a scheme that repeats itself time after time after time, and each time it happens in the same marriage, the unloving is further entrenched.

How about when you rearrange the furniture and he does not notice? Do you feel appreciated and loved? Ooh. Here is a good one. How about when you do the laundry, vacuum the house, clean the kitchen, basically clean the whole house, and he does not even say that it looks nice? He does not thank you and does not recognize the hard work you put in throughout the day. Or when you cook dinner for your family every night, and there is no thank you, and to top it off, you have to clean up by yourself. Do you feel appreciated and loved then? If you say yes, you have either been through healing or you are a liar. Sometimes both. So not only do you feel bad about yourself because of what you believe about yourself and what is said by your spouse to confirm that but also because of what is not said. You see, because past that initial anger of "I cannot believe he did not notice or say thank you," you have the deeper feelings of "I am not worth being noticed and validated with thank you." That, in turn, affects your ability to feel love, which affects your ability to love.

Women are not the only gender that feels bad about themselves when they are not noticed. Men, how do we feel when we work all day long and sometimes pick up an extra job and our wives never seem to notice and say thank you for all of our hard work or appreciate that we are busting our butts for them? How do we feel when we take the time to work out and our wives never mention how we look great? How about when we mow the lawn and take out the trash and there is never a thank you or appreciation showed? Do we feel loved during these times? The problem is when these things happen to make us question if we are loved or not it carries to every other day. After a while we begin to believe that we are not really loved and that we are not even worthy of it.

As long as we are talking about things not being said when we need it, what about those days when we are feeling down about finances, life in general, or ourselves and we really need an encouraging word from our spouses? What happens when we fail to get the encouragement we want? In those times, we really need our spouses to build us up and lift us out of our funk, and we don't get it. We think our spouses should just know when we need them in this way, and when we don't get what we feel we need from them, we don't feel that they care about us. Add that to whatever had us or has us down, and we are in for a pretty rough day.

I used to constantly worry about finances back before God brought me through healing from fear. When I was worrying about the finances, I would look to my wife to tell me everything was going to be okay. I would not tell her I needed her to say that, but I would hope she would. I needed her to pull me out of worry and anxiety. Sometimes she would do that, and sometimes she would not. In the times she didn't, I would get upset, and as an added bonus I would fall into the familiar fear of not being able to provide for my family. This fear would then lead into just how worthless I felt I was, which was a marker on the road to self-hate already existing inside of me. So I was really looking to my wife to make me feel better about myself, and I did not always get that. Even when I did get that, it did not totally take care of that fear. It helped for a little while, but then I would fall right back into that fear and self-hate.

At least we have sex, right? Sex will always make us feel good about ourselves because we will feel wanted and accepted when we are having sex. When we get married, we can have sex whenever we want to, right? So there is something that we could do every day that would make us feel good about ourselves, right?

Has your spouse ever told you that he or she is not in the mood? Have your advances ever been denied? How about that time of the month when you cannot have sex for four or five days? I think that most of us feel some level of rejection when our attempts at sexual intimacy are turned away. I know that my wife would have felt rejected if she was in the mood and I was not. Yes, there were times when I was not in the mood. Crazy, huh? Women, when your husband does not want to have sex, how does that make you feel? Does it make you feel less pretty? Less desirable? Maybe he wants someone else? That would be an ugly lie Satan could throw at you. So the message is "I am gross, ugly, and undesirable." Men, we think that we *deserve* it whenever we want, right? So if she is not in the mood, we feel that she does not respect us men. Or maybe the same ugly lie: "Maybe she wants someone else." So we cannot even count on sex in our marriage to keep us feeling good. So let me ask you, do you really feel good about yourself in your marriage?

It is amazing how much lower the negatives take you compared to the highs of the positives. Is it safe to say that your spouse has never really made you feel good about yourself for more than just a temporary feel-good moment? In fact, if you were asked to remember the last time your spouse said something positive to you that built you up and something negative that tore you down, which one can you remember faster? Which one has stuck with you? Even though you got married to have someone to make you feel good about yourself, do you still walk around most of the time hating yourself and looking for ways to make yourself feel good?

I did a search for "Does your spouse make you feel good?" on Google, and here are some of the responses:

> Not as often as I would like him too—actually I have to ask him how do I look and I tell him why don't you ever tell me I look nice and he says he does but it's funny because I never hear him say it. I am a very confident woman with a very high self esteem and I really don't need him to tell me—but it would make me feel good if he did—but you can't have it all right.

I like this comment because I see a common scheme in it. This woman's husband probably does tell her that she looks nice, but she is not hearing it. She is not receiving it. She claims to be very confident and have a very high self-esteem, but I question that. I used to tell my wife that she was beautiful all the time, but she never received it, and she might say that she never heard me say it.

> Compliments are probably a lot less the longer your married just because you fall into repetition if you do it every day and it would mean less and less. Still even after 9 years I would say we complement each other a couple of times a week over various things.

So what you have to look forward to as you spend more and more years together are less and less compliments. A bright future.

> My Husband rarely compliments ME He compliments my cooking, how clean the house is. Try not to focus on the thought of the compliment, and think about maybe why you need to hear compliments. It doesn't bother me. I compliment my Husband all the time, he is gorgeous. He was skinny and not that attractive when we met, then I fell in love, cooked him good meals for a year, he filled out and I personally think he is one hot 44 year old. Oh, sometimes he says "you have beautiful skin" If I change my hair he'll say something, and sometimes, I guess when he's come home from work a little horny he might say "you look very sexy today" in a child-ish voice, but not very often. I don't let it get to me! We are happy, good sex life, good family life.

We can see an expectation we come into marriage with is that our spouses will never stop complimenting us. When the compliments stop, so does our validation. This is why we are constantly disappointed and hurt when we enter marriage look-ing for our spouses to make us feel good about ourselves. When we "need" compliments from our spouses in order to determine our value, we are really going to struggle. We are trying to get our validation tanks filled from sources that have a limited sup-ply. I will tell you one thing: this woman does let it get to her. I think that she wants the compliments but has just learned not to expect them so she will not be hurt anymore when they do not come.

So what are some of those things that we turn to? Well, sex for one takes on a whole different meaning. Instead of sex being what God intended for it to be, we start to use it to feel good. That is pure selfishness. What else do we turn to? Work? We are not getting the validation from our spouse, so we turn to work to fulfill that need. We pour ourselves into our work. We want to be the best so that we will be worth something. If we are good at our jobs, then we are good people. How about TV? Is that a nice distraction to make you forget that you hate yourself? We can escape into TV. Get lost in it. Imagine our lives are like what we see. When we are in that place, we do not have to deal with the real issues.

What about money? Can you find self-worth in money? Of course you can. If you have money, then you are worth something. People will pay attention to you if you have money. You can have anything you want and people will accept you, right? I know my wife did not marry me for money. I hope she did not marry me on potential to have lots of money either because that isn't going to happen. How about alcohol and drugs? They make you feel good, right? They would take away your pain at least for a little while before they dump more pain on you than you had to begin with.

We also turn to other people. We are not being validated at home, so let's go find it in someone else. I remember that I used to walk into a room and count how many women looked over to check me out. My validation was in that. If I was leaving a place, I could take one of two routes that led to the exit. One way took me behind the place where lots of women were, and the other led me right through them. Well, I would take the path that led right through them so I could see how many were interested in looking at me. It made me feel good about myself. That is a dangerous road to walk. When we start to seek validation and feelings of self-worth from men and women, we are taking a huge risk. It is a slippery slope pointing down to unfaithfulness. It is not just the opposite gender that we seek validation from outside of the marriage, is it? We also have our friends of the same gender that can become entangled in our feelings of self-worth. I am sure if we took a couple minutes to think about it, we could all identify some people in our lives that seem to suck the life out of us. It's because they are trying to pull their value out of us. I can identify some people like that, and I have also been that person. It's not easy to be friends with people like that.

The problem is that all of the other things that we seek "good feeling" in eventually fail. So not only are we shocked that we are married and still hate ourselves, but we cannot find anything that will make us feel good about ourselves. So we get married to have someone who can make us feel good about ourselves, right? I heard a pretty good joke the other day that fits in here.

> A woman was looking in the mirror one morning, and she says that she looks old and tired. She comments on her wrinkles and says that she is getting fat. So she looks at her husband who is sitting on the bed and says, "Can you please say something nice about me?" So he looks at her and says, "You have excellent eyesight."

Well, I guess the question is, do you ever feel rejected by your spouse? Let's take that a step deeper and ask the question have you and do you always feel rejected on some level by your spouse? I would suspect that if you really get honest with yourself, the answer to both of these questions is going to be yes. So if you cannot even expect for your spouse to make you feel good about yourself, then what's the point of getting married? If I am going to be in a relationship with someone who makes me feel bad about myself, I do not need to be married. I can find that in any relationship.

. . .

From Kara:

So this chapter definitely hits home for me. I am not sure it was a primary reason that I got married, but it was certainly a subconscious thought in my mind. I figured that if I was feeling ugly or dumb or whatever that Jesse would be there to constantly build me up and tell me otherwise. Again, I was looking to Jesse to meet an expectation that only God can meet. As I began to deal with the unloving spirit that had plagued my life, I went to Scripture to find out who I truly was and am. God says that I (and all of you) am beautiful, a treasure, his child, a princess, pure, holy, blameless, lovely, and the list goes on ... Now if God, the creator of the universe, thinks that I am all of these amazing things, then who the heck cares what anybody else thinks? Easier said than done, right? This takes constantly replacing those "other thoughts" with the truth, and one day you will not have any problem accepting who you really are in Christ.

One problem with all of this hating yourself business is that Satan is super sneaky! Before walking through any sort of healing for past issues, I would have never said that I hated myself. Sure, like Jesse said earlier, I would walk past a mirror and immediately notice *only* the icky things, but I felt that I was a fairly confident person. It wasn't until I began going through ministry and started recognizing the lies that I believed about myself for what they truly were that I realized that I had a problem. It is *not* normal and it is *not* okay to believe that you are a bad person or that you are unattractive and worthless. God is madly in love with you, and it is not until you fully grasp this that you will be able to begin to love yourself. No amount of compliments or building up from man will change who you believe you are.

* * *

I am not saying that it is wrong for us to compliment our spouses. In fact, when we compliment our spouses without any attempt at manipulation, I believe we are allowing God to speak through us. So those compliments are actually coming from God, and he is using our spouses to speak them to us. However, when we expect our spouses to make us feel good about ourselves, we are setting ourselves up for disappointment. So what's the point?

Money and Provision

I said earlier thank God that my wife did not marry me for money or for even the potential for me to make lots of money. I just do not see that in our future. I hope she doesn't, or there is going to be lots of disappointment.

We find a lot of our security in money, don't we? And why shouldn't we? After all, it allows us to eat and have a place of shelter, right? We all desire security. The desire to feel secure has been formed in us by God. The problem is that we have done an outstanding job of messing up that desire by trying to have other things, instead of God, fulfill it.

It's the security we believe money provides that drives us to try to find a spouse who can earn an adequate living. To gain a little perspective, we would say that the CEO of a large corporation holds significantly more marriage potential than the homeless person on the street. Can we all agree on that? How much more attractive do people get when we know they are loaded or have great jobs? How much more attractive do they get when we conclude they are going to be able to take care of us financially and that we will never have to worry about money? They become a lot more attractive, right? You might say, "Well, I would never marry someone who is living on the street and eating food from the dumpster because there is no way I would be provided for." That is just common sense, right? What if that person on the street is living in faith and trust in the Lord, and God is taking him/her through a season of total provision coming from God in weird ways? So this person on the street is actually getting it right. You would be more provided for in that relationship than any other because God is the one providing there, and he never fails. I don't need to look very far to see the relevance of this in my own life.

I grew up in a home where the woman was career-oriented. It is true that society is more like this today than it has ever been, but my home was a shining example of how the woman can help the financial climate by working. My mother felt that it was important for her to have a career. There were many things reinforcing the importance of her job, including identity, self-worth, and so on. However, those things didn't matter to me. What stuck with me was that in order to survive in this day and age, the home had to be supported with a dual income.

When I met Kara she was a head lifeguard. I was impressed with the ambition in her to "climb the ladder" so to speak. I could see that she was a very smart girl and that, if she wanted to, she could rise to the top in whatever field she chose. This was very attractive to me because she was displaying the qualities I believed a woman should have.

We got married, and in the first years of our marriage, she held a couple of different jobs. It amazed me that wherever she was they wanted to promote and move her up. What amazed me even more was that she continued to turn them down. I thought she was crazy. It didn't make any sense to me. Why in the world would someone turn down a promotion? When I asked her she would just say, "I don't have any desire to become a career-oriented person. What I really want to be is a stay-at-home mom."

I had no grid of understanding for an answer like the one she gave me. On the surface it produced a lot of confusion. Underneath the confusion, resentment and bitterness were breeding. I thought I had married someone who was going to help me maintain our standard of living, and instead I was face-to-face with the possibility I was going to have to do it all myself. I began to look down on her. You have to understand that much of my identity and worth was wrapped up in her. If she went out and succeeded in the workplace, then I was a success. If she didn't then I was unsuccessful. Can you relate to this? We want to feel that our spouses are worthy providers so there is pride when we talk about what our spouses do. I began to resent my wife because I felt that she was taking me down with her. It sounds ridiculous and ugly, but most of our perceptions born from pain and wounds are, in fact, ridiculous and ugly.

I had married a woman I believed was going to make me feel more secure financially. Instead, I felt like the carpet was pulled out from under me and everything landed on my shoulders. I'm sure you can understand the destructive dynamic this created in our marriage relationship.

Many of us have had the perceived security of well-providing spouses ripped away in an instant. It doesn't matter if it's ripped away because of disability, layoffs, or general apathy toward work altogether. Many of us have allowed the security of a provider to influence our decision to get married. When we get married to people we feel have displayed the qualities of a great provider, we feel secure. When that security is ripped away for any reason, we feel betrayed, angry, bitter, and resentful.

It wasn't too long before debt started to pile up on us. I blamed myself for that, but there was also a piece of me that blamed her as well. If she was working then we would not have had to go into debt for the things we wanted. I know there are many things wrong with that last statement. As debt increased I felt more and more like a failure.

So one of the reasons that we are getting married is based on the potential person's ability to provide financially. Let us look at this from two different angles. The first is going to be money in general, and the second will be your spouse's ability to provide it.

Money

> For the love of money is the root of all evil: which while some coveted after, they have erred from the faith, and pierced themselves through with many sorrows.
>
> 1 Timothy 6:10

Money seems to be one of the top priorities in any marriage relationship. It is the most talked about issue, and it wears many different masks. It is without a doubt the number one cause of fear, anxiety, worry, dread, stress, bitterness, and resentment in marriage relationships.

The roots of most money issues in marriage relationships are selfishness and a sense of entitlement. We have decided to marry people who can give us the most financial security, and with it we carry an interesting expectation. We expect to have exclusive rights to the money coming into our home. For those of us who are providing the income, we feel entitled to it because we are the ones earning it. For those of us who married a provider, we feel entitled to it because it's our provision. There is something inside of us all that tells us we are the ones who should have the final say in what the money buys and where it goes. There is very little compromise, and in the end, though there may be initial discussion, there is one person who will say, "This is how it is going to be."

For most of my marriage I have been the provider. I have earned the majority of the income. With that knowledge came a sense of authority and exclusive right to do whatever I wanted with the money I had earned. I remember many times Kara and I would discuss different money-related things, and though I carried on a discussion with her, it was really just a formality. We both knew, in many cases, that I was eventually going to do what I thought was the right thing.

It wasn't very often that I thought, *Do we have the money for this right now?* before making a purchase. But when Kara wanted to buy something, that question was always asked. The result was a seed of resentment planted in Kara.

We have decided to marry people who can provide for us, but when those providers feel they have the right to control the money, it breeds anger, bitterness, and resentment. We married these people for security, but instead fear and uncertainty come to life because we are not allowed to be a part of any financial decisions.

What's the point of marrying people for financial security and then not having any rights, let alone exclusive rights, to the income?

Spouse's Ability to Provide Money

So this is where we have put our security: in our spouse's ability to provide for us financially. We seek peace in that. I mean, we would not have married our spouses if we thought they were dead beats, right? And now, for some of us, we are feeling secure because our spouses have great jobs, and in some cases both spouses have great jobs. We have good income coming in, so we are doing okay, right?

The national unemployment rate at the time of this writing is nine percent. There many families with no main source of income. There are many spouses right now without any way to support their families. There are probably lots of spouses who feel let down by a spouse who formally provided but is now unable to produce income.

People, jobs are fickle. Do you think you have job security? I would encourage you to evaluate that. Things can always change. There was a chance that I was going to get laid off from the fire department because of property tax cuts that deeply affected civil services. Lots of firefighters in the state of Florida have been laid off along with many other government workers. We are on shaky ground right now, but the economy is not the only reason why jobs are fickle. What if you get a boss who does not like you and wants you out? Some bosses can make that happen, right? Do you ever feel like you are just one mistake away from being replaced? I have felt that way before.

Those of you who own a small business know how difficult it is to be successful. Fifty percent of start-up small businesses fail in the first five years. Even well-established business can go belly up in what seems like an instant. Enron collapsed and left many people out of work and unable to provide for their families. Many people who got married with the notion that they would be provided for the rest of their life by their spouse would be very disappointed.

Another thing that makes jobs fickle is our own health. According to howstuffworks.com, in 2004 fifty-six billion dollars was paid out in workman's comp benefits. That is a lot of money and should tell you something about the certainty you have that you are going to be healthy enough to do your job. Also, a pay cut comes with receiving workman's comp. Unless you have supplemental disability insurance, you are going to have to live on less than what you were. Do you all realize that your spouse could go to work one day, get hurt, and never be able to do that same job or even work again? You say, "Well, I trust God will keep my spouse safe." Guess what: there are lots of Christians out there who have been hurt or killed at their place of employment, leaving their spouses with no one to provide for them, so let me ask you, what are you doing that they were not that makes you so sure God will protect your spouse? Are you reading your Bible more or praying harder than them? Are you living a more righteous lifestyle than them?

Does God offer us protection? Absolutely! Does it have anything to do with how much we read our Bibles or pray? I don't believe it does. Does it depend on the choices we make? You bet it does.

The point is that we really don't understand our spouse's ability to provide for us can be so quickly taken away and frequently is. We push that thought out of our mind because I mean, really, what are we supposed to do with that? How are we supposed to entertain that thought? We are not supposed to entertain that thought because it brings fear, worry, stress, dread, and anxiety, and all of those things are ungodly.

Let's talk a minute about illegal activities. Have you ever found out that your spouse was providing for you by engaging in illegal activities? Did you care? Maybe not, but I am assuming that the vast majority of you would have a problem with your spouse being a criminal. It would be hard for your spouse to provide for you from prison. I know of a woman who got married, and a big reason for marrying was because he could provide for her. Well, a couple of years later, she found out that her spouse was making money illegally. That hurt and wounded her deeply; she felt betrayed and stupid. It took a long time for her to heal from that wound.

Money is also one of the leading causes of divorce today. That is not hard to understand. Arguments about how it should be spent can get pretty heated. Marriage is also stressed when there is no money and you do not know how you are going to make it. Why does that matter to us? Well, because the reason we got married was so we could have someone to provide for us, and if our spouses are not doing that, then they are not living up to their end of the bargain.

So where exactly are you trying to plant your feet here? You cannot trust or depend on money, you cannot trust that your spouse will always be able to provide money, and money in and of itself has the ability to destroy your marriage. So if it is impossible to know that the person you are going to marry or are married to is going to provide for you for the rest of your life, then what is or what was the point of getting married?

Sex

We love sex. I remember clearly the anticipation I had for sex when I got engaged. It was always something that I looked forward to. I had believed and accepted that sex before marriage is fornication, and so I did not do it. I was looking forward to marriage because it would allow me to have sex for the first time. I don't really think it matters regarding anticipation whether or not you are a virgin when you get married. Even if you have already had sex before you get married, you are still looking forward to it with your spouse. Maybe you are even looking forward to being able to do it without having to feel guilty afterwards. I remember some of the things I thought. I was going to be able to do it whenever I wanted, my wife was going to want to do it all of the time, and it was going to make me feel great. I don't remember if I put a number to the amount of sex that I was going to have per week, but I remember feeling like it would be every day. I found out that was not very realistic. Some couples have sex every day. More power to them. It is not a reality in my house, and that is okay.

My wedding night was great, but it was not what I expected. There is that old expectation thing again bringing disappointment. I actually wanted to order a pizza as soon as we got to the hotel. My wife still gives me a hard time about that. I was really hungry. Don't get me wrong, it was great, but not what I thought it would be. I had a picture in my head of volcanic eruptions and geysers bursting. I thought that everything I knew would be turned upside down when I had sex for the first time. I thought everything else would pale in comparison. I thought the world would stop just for us, that the passion would be indescribable. I thought that Kara and I would feel this incredible connection as we became one flesh. Those things did happen to a degree but not to the degree that I thought they would. What I know now is that we were getting it wrong. No, not mechanically (come on now), but spiritually and emotionally.

Sex was created and instituted by God. When it happens within the parameters of a marriage relationship, it can be one of the most amazing experiences we can have as humans. You may have noticed I said "It *can* be." Many people teach that the only thing we need for godly sex is marriage. I am here to tell you there is much more involved in sanctifying sex than just a couple of rings.

It is not wrong to want to be married so that we can enjoy sex. However, we, as followers of Jesus, must consider the possibility that our godly desires have taken on ungodly properties. Look at it this way. The Bible says that we are slaves, right? We are slaves to sin or slaves to righteousness. Either way we are slaves, and we only have a choice of two masters. We can choose to serve God, or we can choose to serve Satan. So in that perspective, everything we do is an act of service to whomever we have decided to serve. If you do not prayerfully commit your sexual intimacy to God, who do you think you are serving with it?

Satan uses sex to hold so many people in bondage. There is

so much sexual immorality in the world today. If Satan can gain a right to use it in your life, you can bet that he will. We talked earlier about Satan using anything and everything he can to destroy intimacy. If he can extract God from our sexual intimacy, he has destroyed our ability to be intimate in the most powerful way God has given us. The reason is that through making love, we have the ability not only to touch our spouses' souls in the most powerful way but also to touch the heart of God in ways unavailable through anything else. If Satan can destroy this he has gained victory in our marriage relationships and the path to destruction has been opened. So let's discuss some of the ways our godly intentions have become ungodly.

Pornography is not only an issue in individuals but is also an issue in marriage relationships. Many Christian couples have not only engaged in watching pornography together but have embraced it as something that has helped their marriages. Most of you don't need an explanation of why this is wrong. For those who do, here are a couple of reasons.

> You are watching people commit fornication, promote homo-sexual activity, and committing adultery. Just by watching this you are coming into agreement that it's okay.

> It is impossible to watch pornography and stay free from lust. For those of you saying "Yes it is," no, it's not. Lust is the same as committing adultery, right? Essentially you are committing adultery right in front of your spouse.

Another issue to be addressed is the use of sex toys. Why is it that we always feel like we need to enhance pleasure? What a lie from Satan. It's the lie that says we can take something given by God and make it better. Where did we ever get the right to think and act this way? Don't we believe that things which are God-given, by their very nature, are the very best we can ever hope to experience? If sex is boring for you, then instead of bringing in toys, I would suggest asking God if you are getting it right or if there is something defiling it. Also consider that if you are bringing sex toys into your relationships, the focus is most likely on you and your spouse, and God has been disregarded. What a great idea. Disregard the one who gave us sex in the first place.

What is the draw of role playing? There could be some similarities between role playing and sex toys in the fact that they are both sought to increase pleasure. What is the illusion of role playing? You are pretending that your spouse is a completely different person, right? Somebody please tell me the difference between this and committing adultery. Yes, it is really your spouse, but if you are seeing someone different in your mind, then it's adultery. Why isn't your spouse enough for you? You may say, "He/she is enough for me." Obviously not because in an effort to prevent sex from becoming boring you have to pretend he/she is someone else. That's a problem that needs a solution. Again, most likely if you are engaging in role playing God has been disregarded and self ambitions have been elevated.

Selfishness. Selfishness is something that will suck godliness right out of our sexual intimacy quickly and effectively. It can manifest in a couple different ways. Some of them are very subtle. As we talk about this, recognize that selfishness is typically something that we sense in sexual intimacy. Most of us are not going to say to our spouses that our goal is to make sure we are pleasured first. If selfishness is an issue, it will be felt, and we may not know how to explain something is wrong but we know something is.

Selfishness can manifest with the resolution we are not going to stop until we reach orgasm and if we don't then it was a failed session. Should the number one priority of making love be to reach orgasm or to connect with the hearts of God and our spouses? Yes, orgasm is important, but when it consumes our intentions, it is a problem.

Selfishness can also manifest in a more subtle way. Many of us get our validation and worth from sexual intimacy. There are people who would say "When we make love my attention is on my spouse. I don't think about myself. My number one priority is to make sure my spouse is pleasured." That sounds very noble. In fact, that is exactly the same attitude that I had, so I will speak this from personal experience. Even though my attention was on my wife, I received much of my validation as a man and worth as a husband on my ability to pleasure my wife sexually. So as I pleasured my wife I was receiving validation and worth. I was only giving so that I could get. It's selfishness, and it undermines the godliness of sex.

All of these are ways that Satan is given access to our marriage relationships. When he gets in he uses these things to turn our godly intentions into sin and destruction. The very reasons that drive us into marriage, though godly, can be the very same things Satan uses to destroy our marriages. Why is pleasure automatically defined by sex toys, role playing, and any other enhancers? I guarantee you that when the ungodliness is extracted from your sexual intimacy the pleasure you experience will be far greater you ever imagined or hoped it could be.

There are actually a lot of people out there who say that sex gets worse when you get married. I am sure you have all heard the jokes about how seldom married people have sex. I have heard many men complain about how little they "get it." So it begs the question how often are you having sex? According to the *Newsweek* article called "No sex please. We're Married," 10–15 percent of couples are having sex no more than ten times a year. That is a large number of couples who are having sex less than once per month. That is enough to make you say, "That cannot be true." Or maybe you are saying, "That is pretty accurate." No matter what side you are on, I would bet that if you are on the "cannot be true" side, you cannot imagine how your sex life could get there, and if you are on the other side, you are wondering, *How in the world did we get here?* You probably never would have thought before you got married that years down the road you would only be having sex once a month. I read a comment online that a couple that had only been married for four years was only having sex once a month if he was lucky.

This article also suggested that the stereotype of women being the ones that decline sex is wrong. It suggests that men are more likely to decline sex than women. Is that easy for you to accept? I can honestly say that I do not want to have sex all of the time. I have declined sex over the years. So has my wife. I cannot say that one of us has declined it more than the other, but what I probably could say is that it seems, for both of us, that it is the other person who has declined it more often.

This article states that married people for the first year are having sex an average of three times a week. Is that more or less than you expected? I would imagine you would say you expected that number to be higher. The normal pattern of thought is that at first the number is very high, and then it gradually drops down and levels out. Well, the surveys done for this article show that couples admit that they are having sex one or two times a week. So it starts at three and then drops to once or twice. Is that what you thought it would be before you got married? Many of us, before we get married, expect those numbers to be five to seven times a week and then drop to three times a week. I looked at another Web site called professorhouse.com, and the study there showed that married couples are having sex an average of two times a week. I can say that my wife and I are intimate two or three times a week, but I always felt that I was on the lower end of the average.

So how many times do you and your spouse have sex throughout the week? Does it line up with what these sources say is "average"? Let me also ask you if you wish you were having sex more than what you are. You know what is strange is that even though I do not have a desire to have sex with my wife every day, in the past I have wished that I was doing it every day. There is an underlying tone to marriage that says your marriage is only as good as how often you are having sex. If you are only having sex once a week, then your marriage is in trouble.

Think about it and be honest. If it has been a week since you and your spouse had sex, do you think that you are still as close as you should be? Do you get anxious and nervous and say to yourself that you better have sex soon so things can be right? There is a pressure to make sure you are having sex regularly. Society has built that pressure, and Hollywood has shown us that what makes a good relationship is good sex. Well, it is impossible to have good sex if you are not having sex at all, so then the next thought is that your relationship is no good.

Have you ever had the "How many times do you guys have sex a week?" conversation with other married friends? Of course you have, and isn't there always something in you that makes you want to outdo your friend? Of course there is. Whenever someone asks us that question, don't we think of a week where we had sex an unusual amount of times and say that is the norm? Oh, and if we are having sex twice a week, we are going to say when asked that we are having sex two to three times a week. So do you wish that you were having sex more often? You probably do. Why is that?

Do you think there is something wrong with you if you do not want to have sex every day? For men there is more pressure to want sex every day. The problem is that most of us do not want it every day, and the image that society has built is that if you were a real man or in a healthy relationship, you would be having sex all the time.

I remember that I got married around the time when erectile dysfunction drugs were pretty big. I was actually concerned that there was something medically wrong with me and that there might be some dysfunction because I did not want to have sex every single day. All that does is add fear, stress, worry, and dread. Oh, and anxiety that if I do not have sex with my wife enough then she would cheat on me or leave me. That is not a fun road to go down. So, yeah, we feel there is something wrong with us if we do not want to have sex more often than we are. So how much is enough to make you feel that you are a real, healthy man? It would be impossible for you to have enough sex to fulfill those needs.

Is the amount of sex you and your spouse are having directly related to how much he or she still desires you? That would make sense, would it not? The best way our spouses can show that they still desire us is to have sex with us, right? So is two times a week enough to let you know that you are still the only one your spouse desires? That would mean that twice a week for a short amount of time would be the only times that you know your spouse still desires you. I do not think that is enough. So the rest of the week you wonder if you are enough for him or her. God forbid you miss one time and only have sex once that week. Now your spouse desires you half as much, right? So again we ask the question how much is enough? Is it possible to have sex enough to give you the constant feeling that you are still desirable and the only one for your spouse? You really need to think about that, and when you admit that it is not possible, you can then open yourself up to allow God to get in there and bring healing. I am not saying that you do not need sex, but I am saying that if you are putting your idea of how much your spouse desires you in how often you have sex, you are going to be feeling pretty insecure in your marriage and bad about yourself most of the time.

So when you break it down, you are having sex to feel good about yourself, make sure that your spouse still desires you, maintain expectations, and make sure that there is nothing physically wrong with you. This is beginning to sound more and more like sex is a chore and not anything close to what you thought it would be. You have to do it to maintain all of the above. How many of us feel that way? It is hard work trying to have sex enough to maintain all of those things. The funny thing is that those things are never maintained for long. Here is a definition of insanity: "Doing the same thing over and over again and expecting different results." I see that applying to the way we approach sex in marriage. We are all insane. As an added bonus, we have taken what started as a godly desire and allowed all sorts of ungodliness into it. What was supposed to be one of the best parts of marriage is actually killing our relationships. It is okay, though, because God heals.

A friend of mine brought up the following passages as being very relevant to this chapter. There are some things in sexual intimacy that we can look to Scripture and find verses that say, in a very black and white way, they are wrong. There are other things that Scripture does not address specifically, and so we are left to try to justify them by what we know to be true about who God is and his character and by revelation that he brings to us. So for those issues that can be a toss up, consider the following:

> "Everything is permissible"—but not everything is beneficial. "Everything is permissible"—but not everything is constructive.
>
> 1 Corinthians 10:23 (NIV)

> "Everything is permissible for me"—but not everything is beneficial. "Everything is permissible for me"—but I will not be mastered by anything.
>
> 1 Corinthians 6:12 (NIV)

These are great because Paul is giving us a standard to live by when our questions are not specifically addressed in the Bible. Everything is permissible, but not everything is okay and godly. The question we have to ask when it comes to gray areas regarding sexual intimacy is, "is what we are doing beneficial and constructive?" For whom is it supposed to be beneficial and constructive? The answer to that question is God first and foremost, and then to us individually. You really only need to answer the first question because if what we are doing is not beneficial to God and his purpose, then there is no chance that it is beneficial and constructive to us individually.

You may say as you ponder this, "Well, it is not exactly beneficial and constructive to God, but we also cannot see any negative side to it as well, so it really seems neutral." There is nothing that we do on this earth that is neutral. Everything we do serves one of two kingdoms. There is nothing, and I mean nothing, we do or don't do in our lives that does not weigh in one kingdom or the other. There is not one time that Jesus implies that neutral is an option for us. We are either for him or against him. There is no middle ground.

. . .

From Kara:

Some may adamantly disagree with this chapter and say that anything goes as long as my spouse and I agree. I would like to simply ask that you prayerfully consider the possibility that you may be in error. Jesse and I went through a time where we tampered in some gray areas. After the times that we did this, I would feel icky and certainly not holy. It was nothing more than having worldly sex. Love was not involved; it was all about lust.

We are no longer interested in allowing anything ungodly to enter into our marriage, and gray areas are a wide open door for that to happen. Something you may want to try is praying before making love. I know this may sound weird—I thought so too at first—but it really allows God to truly be at the center of everything you do. Just *try* it!

. . .

So to wrap this up: You got married to have sex. Great! You got married so that ten to fifteen percent of you can have sex just ten times a year and the rest of us one to two times a week. You also do not have it enough to feel good about yourself or to make sure your spouse still desires you. It has also been the reason that you may have thought there is something physically wrong with you. It has become boring, and you have resorted to sinful practices and things that God never wanted to make it exciting. This, as a result, makes you feel even worse about yourself. You know that there should be something more to it, but you do not know what or how to get there. You feel obligated to do it, and it leaves you feeling empty a lot of the time. It has also become a chore. So with all of this, what is the point of getting married? I mean good grief. You can be in sin, have bad sex, and hate yourself without being married.

?

Building a Family

I remember back when I was young saying that I wanted to get married and have kids. Actually, out of all the reasons to get married, this one speaks the most to me. It has just always been a strong desire in me. It is going to be a little painful for me to break this one down, but here we go.

Like many of the previous reasons, God has placed the desire to have and to build a family in us. However, just like many of the previous reasons, Satan has done a good job of twisting and manipulating this desire and has brought some negative things from it.

I grew up a very sensitive kid. When I got older, I rejected sensitivity because I viewed it as weakness, but I am getting back to that now, glory to God. I say this because I did not have a one-track mind growing up. Sure, I thought about sex often, but that did not motivate me in relationships. I was always interested in long-term potential. I wanted something deep in a relationship. I wanted more than just physical. I guess it is the way I am wired.

So I guess it makes sense that I grew up desiring to get married for the purpose of building a family. I had it all planned out. I would have a boy and a girl. I would raise them, and they would grow up to be successful and it would be a rewarding experience. Well, praise God I have a boy and a girl, and they are very rewarding. I do not know what they are going to be when they grow up, but I entrust them to the Lord. There is just something that tugs on my spirit when I think about raising a family with a beautiful wife. It is what I have always wanted.

The things we experience growing up or the way marriage was modeled to us plays a significant role in what reasons we choose to get married. I, for example, grew up in a home where marriage and family worked. While I was in my family system, everything seemed to flow together seamlessly. My parents did fight and argue in front of us, but there was always reconciliation. I was brought up in a system where marriage and family worked, so it is not a stretch that this would be a significant reason that I would want to be married. I knew in my knower that I wanted a family like I grew up in, and I also knew that did not come without marriage for me. The thought that I could have a family without being married did not occur to me. Many people can and have built a family without being married, but that was just not in my framework to consider. In fact, if I would have gotten a girl pregnant, I am sure that theology would have pushed me to get married to that person.

So as I moved out of that family dynamic and into my own dynamic with my wife, I tried to duplicate my experience growing up. That almost immediately was destroyed as the first couple years of my marriage I did not speak to my parents. There were some destructive and divisive things that happened between me, my older sister and her husband, and my younger sister that pitted my older sister and me against my younger sister and my parents. That was a very painful time, and that story could fill another book. Glory to God for the healing and reconciliation that has been done with my family, and we are all enjoying relationship today. That is a miracle in itself.

As I navigated through this painful time in my life, God brought some revelations I had not been able to see before. My family dynamic growing up was far from perfect. There was real dysfunction there. I came to realize that just because you know you are loved by your parents and that they love each other, it doesn't necessarily mean you are growing up in the healthiest environment. I am not saying that as I looked back I realized my upbringing was awful. I do not think that in the slightest, but I do look back and see there was pain there. Things were not as perfect and healthy as I thought they were while growing up in it. I will not go into all of the problems here, but the most damaging thing that came out of it was that I had developed expectations about what raising a family would be like. All of them positive. I would challenge anyone who grew up in a family that seemed to work perfectly to consider what I have said and ask yourself what expectations you had about building a family and how those expectations have been destroyed over the years.

On the flip side, I would fully expect that those of you who were brought up in a broken family, where there was not even the sense of healthy relationships, to have gotten or to want to be married for different reasons. Why would you have a strong desire to build a family after the one you were in was filled with pain and brokenness? Let me share an example from a friend of mine I thought challenged this point of view.

Like many of us, this person had come from an unhealthy family life. Her parents never divorced, but the threat was mentioned many times. She was never physically abused; however, her siblings were. There were days of screaming, ripping phones from the wall, and throwing whatever was in reach. Then there were days of happiness and what some would call love. The environment was unstable and very volatile. After sharing this, the question "Why did you get married?" came up, and she said because she wanted to have a family. That made me scratch my head a little because it really challenged my perspective on this matter.

After asking her to explain a little more, we came to this revelation. When we grow up in an environment that is not healthy but is the only one we know, it's going to seem normal to us. My friend said it was only in looking back, as she has grown closer to God, that she realized she had grown up in an unhealthy environment. However, as she grew up in that environment, it was normal to her, so why wouldn't she have a strong desire to have a family of her own? It's no surprise that the boys she dated generally had anger issues similar to her father, but as she grew spiritually she realized that God's idea of marriage was different than her own and much healthier. Today she has been happily married for eleven years to a man who wants God at the center of their marriage as much or more than she does. They have found that loving Jesus more than each other is what makes it peaceful, loving, stable, and healthy.

So what I wanted to point out is for those of you who know people who have grown up in a broken environment but who still seem to have a great desire to build a family, it does not disprove my perspective on this matter. If you come from a home where there is divorce, abuse, or some other tragedy that is very damaging, that is when a person might start searching for other reasons to get married.

The thing that I failed to realize is how hard it was going to be. I never thought about that. I guess whenever I thought about raising a family it was all positive and never negative. Raising a family has not gone as I planned. Over the years, there has been pain I never thought I would know personally, my kids have not always responded the way I thought they would, and there have been times I was sure I was a pretty crappy father. There were also many times I felt my kids loved my wife more than me. To sum it all up in a phrase, there are very few things that have happened as I imagined they would. It has made me wonder at times, *What's the point?*

I know I am not the only one who always desired to have and raise a family as the primary reason they got married. Another friend of mine also shared this desire. What I believe happens when we come into marriage with this desire is that we come into it with unrealistic expectations. For example, "All I have to do is just get married and have kids, and the rest will take care of itself." Or "If I can just get married and have a family, I will always be happy." How about "My kids will be great, and there will never be any conflict between us"? I came into marriage with some of these expectations and beliefs, and to tell you the truth, there are times I see the freedom that other people have who do not have kids and envy them. Sometimes I feel trapped, and that really messes me up because if I got married so that I could have a family and then there are times that I wonder what it would be like not to have one, why did I get married?

Now don't get me wrong. I love my kids and cannot imagine life without them. Well, actually, I just said that I can imagine life without them, didn't I? Let me rephrase that. I do not want things to be different, and if I could go back in time, I would not change anything. My kids are an incredible blessing. I just need to change my perspective because my old belief was that I would never be tired of them, and that is just not the case.

Pregnancy Problems

Let's talk about some other things that my caused my perspective to change. Let's talk about some things that directly affect the desire to build a family. How about pregnancy problems? My wife started to go into labor at thirty-four weeks with my son. We went to the hospital, and they were able to stop the contractions. Kara was in the hospital for two weeks just lying there. It was very frustrating for her and for me. I could not be there with her all of the time. I had to work. I was very concerned that my son would be born early and have a whole truck-load of medical problems. Kara gave birth at thirty-six weeks and everything was fine.

Two years later Kara was pregnant again and started to have contractions at thirty-three weeks. We went through the same thing again, but this time Kara was on bed rest at home for two weeks, and then she had to go in to the hospital for one week. Again, I was worried that my daughter was going to be born early and have a bunch of medical problems. Well, Kara gave birth to my daughter at thirty-six weeks and everything was fine.

Now I do know that there are pregnancy problems that make what I have experienced seem like a piece of cake. What about things like stillborn babies and eclampsia, pre-eclampsia, cords around the neck, pregnancy-induced diabetes? Then you also have things like breech delivery and c-section and premature delivery. There are many more potential complications to pregnancy. Many are life threatening not only to your child but also to you. Did you think about these things when you desired to build a family? I did not. Here are some statistics from www.americanpregnancy.org:

There are approximately 6 million pregnancies every year throughout the United States:

- 4,058,000 live births
- 1,995,840 pregnancy losses

Every year in the United States there are approximately 2 million women who experience pregnancy loss:

- 600,000 women experience pregnancy loss through miscarriage
- 1,200,000 women experience pregnancy loss through termination
- 64,000 women experience pregnancy loss through ectopic pregnancy

- 6,000 women experience pregnancy loss through molar pregnancies
- 26,000 women experience pregnancy loss through stillbirth

Every year in the United States:

- 875,000 women experience one or more pregnancy complications
- 458,952 babies are born to mothers without adequate pre-natal care
- 467,201 babies are born prematurely
- 307,030 babies are born with low birth weight
- 154,051 children are born with birth defects
- 27,864 infants die before their first birthday

These statistics are a little disturbing. Actually, it is very disturbing to know that one-third of all pregnancies will be lost. Then, with the remaining children, there are so many that experience serious problems. I am sure that if you have healthy children you will be thanking God a little more after looking at those statistics. I definitely will be.

Having the chance to walk through some of the problems with preterm labor was enough to recognize the torment of fear as it took my mind captive. Add to it the fact that my wife was unable to take care of herself as she was confined to bed rest and we are talking about loads of stress and anxiety joining the mix. I am sure that many of you who have been involved in the statistics I mentioned earlier would join me in saying, "This isn't what I signed up for."

Will I Be a Good Father/Mother?

Okay, so we have dealt with pregnancy problems. Let's talk a little about the fear that comes during pregnancy and after that you are going to be a bad father or mother. At what point do we realize that we have absolutely no idea what the heck we are doing? For me it was after my son was born in the hospital. I felt like a child with a little baby. I questioned that I had enough responsibility to raise a child. It has definitely been a process.

> But I would have you know, that the head of every man is Christ; and the head of the woman is the man; and the head of Christ is God.
>
> 1 Corinthians 11:3

So here we see godly order. Paul says here that the head of the women is man. So we can say that the head of the family is the man. That is some pressure on us men, is it not? Not only do we have to figure out how we are supposed to raise this child, but we also have to stand up and be the head of the family. If we do a good job and live righteously, then we are blessed, but if we do not, then we have this to look forward to:

> Then I will set my face against that man, and against his family, and will cut him off, and all that go a whoring after him, to commit whoredom with Molech, from among their people.
>
> Leviticus 20:5

So if we live in disobedience, then not only will God set his face against us but also our family. Great! No pressure there. But it is true. Where do you think that generational blessing and curses came from? I am not sure, but if you pass down generational curses, then there may be something to be said about how good of a father you were. Those of us who are so concerned about being great parents and not wanting to have conflict with our children will put up with iniquity and allow the curses to flow downstream. Men seem to have some pretty heavy responsibility in the family dynamic. Let's bring women into the mix and discuss something that affects both genders.

How many of us take our feelings of worth and validation from how good we are as parents? I did. I know I'm not the only one. I held my worth and value against how I was as a father. The problem is it's impossible to be a perfect parent. In my mind, there was always something I could be doing better. I could never live up to my own expectations. The result was a cloud of failure hovering over me. I could never be a good enough father to fill up my validation and worth tank with any lasting results. There were times I would feel like a pretty good dad. For example, my son played flag football, and I made sure I was at his games every Saturday morning. It is important to be at our children's events, whatever they may be. However, it didn't take long for that feeling to leak out of my tank, and before I knew it, I was questioning my worth again.

I have come into contact with many fathers and mothers in ministry. When the questions start to get real and people start to get honest, I find there are very few who actually truly believe they are good parents. Since most of them have tied self-worth to parenting, the result is they also truly believe they are pretty crappy people.

It was an interesting revelation for me to understand one of the biggest reasons I wanted to get married was also one of the biggest reasons I was continually disappointed in myself. It would be silly to think feelings of failure and disappointment as a parent would not leak over into our marriage relationships. Before we know it we are feeling like we have let our spouses down because we can't be the parents we hoped we could be. We feel like if our kids grow up and fall apart, whatever that would look like, it would be our fault. This feeling carries much guilt, shame, and condemnation with it. How do we compensate for that? We pull away. We become less involved because we figure it's better for our kids to spend more time with the better spouse. However, this just brings more guilt, shame, and condemnation. Good grief! No wonder most of us hate ourselves.

There is another interesting perspective in this issue. When we do things for our children—for example, spend time with them, go to their events, read to them, take care of them, praise them, and everything else we think it means to be a good parent—with the motivation being to fill our tanks of validation, approval, acceptance, worth, identity, and, in reality, love, what exactly are we operating in? Is the million-dollar word here selfishness? Many parents think they are doing a great job because they are doing all of the things I listed with and for their children. We think we are operating in love, but we really are operating in selfishness. I did, my wife did, and almost everyone who comes in for ministry is. A good question to ask is "When I don't feel like I am doing a good job with the things listed above, do my tanks seems to run empty?" If the answer is yes, then you are using your children to fill your tanks instead of allowing God to fill them. That is selfishness.

What I understand now is that the best we can do for our children is to ask God to show himself through us. Back when I was trying to be a good parent, I had no idea how to have God shine through me. I didn't even know what that meant. Essentially, I got married with a great passion for family, but I had not the slightest clue how to be a good parent.

That is a lot to think and worry about, is it not? Is it worth the headache?

Kids!

I am sorry. I just have to say it. Sometimes kids can be so annoying! There are times that I feel like I have to just get away. There are so many noises, and it seems that they do not know how to ask a question or just speak anything in an "inside" voice. My son talks to me as if I am across the room even though I am standing right in front of him. I am sure that I have some degree of hearing loss from all the yelling! It is very irritating.

My respect for my wife has grown exponentially because she puts up with it all day long for most days. I get to go to work and have relief. Work sometimes is a vacation for me. That's kind of messed up. She really does not have that. I know that sometimes she wants to just scream.

It is also sometimes annoying to not have the time or freedom to do the things that you want to do. When you have kids, you are not able to do whatever you want to. Someone has to stay at home with the kids. A lot of the time it is not desirable to take the kids with you. So what do you end up doing? Much of the time you end up staying home, or you make your wife or husband stay home with them alone. Of course if you do the latter, you then have to deal with an angry spouse when you get home. It is also annoying to feed them, bathe them, and wipe their butts after they go to the bathroom. I am eagerly awaiting the day when my kids can do all of that stuff without my wife and me.

Kids can also be disrespectful. Why in the world would I ever think that when I tell my kids to do something they would look at me and say "No!" That is just preposterous, right? That does not fit into my idea of a perfect family at all. How much do rude, disrespectful kids damage your desire to have kids or make you question why you even have them? No family is immune to this. I know that we all take notice of a child misbehaving in public, running around and not listening to his or her parents. We all judge that kid and his or her parents, right? It is probably right around that time we should take notice of our own children and try to stop them from doing whatever it is they are doing that they shouldn't be. Now don't get me wrong. I do stand in firm belief that proper disciplining and consistency can prevent and correct much unruly and disrespectful behavior. In fact, I believe that is biblical. However, wouldn't it be nice if our children would just be respectful and do what we tell them to do all the time without question? That would have fit much nicer into my "perfect family" box.

So let's say, for argument's sake, that you raised a perfect family. Your kids were always respectful and had perfect manners. They were never rude, and they always did exactly what you told them to do right away. Guess what. They are still going to leave you. Nearly 100 percent of kids end up leaving their parents' house. Psychology has a term for what can happen to the parents when this happens. It is called the "empty nest" syndrome. It can be very painful and damaging to the parent and our marriage relationships.

Here is another interesting point. Mom, your son is very possibly going to leave you for another woman, and Dad, your daughter is very possibly going to leave you for another man. How have you dealt with that, and for those of us who have not been there yet, how do we think we are going to be able to handle that? My daughter and I are very close. It may be harder for me than I think. The point is that you can do everything right. You can do everything perfectly. Your kids can always make the right choices and never get into trouble. They can always be respectful, and they can still send you into a spiral of depression, sadness, and feelings of betrayal when they leave the house. Is this something we have considered with our desire to build a family?

On top of that, the divorce rate for long-term married couples has been steadily increasing over the last couple of years after the last child leaves the house. I saw this happen with a really good couple friend of my family growing up. Very sad.

Often, as I was growing up, when I would think about having my own family someday, I would seldom think about the day when my kids would leave. Why would I think about that? That would not bring any good feelings. If I got married to build a family, what the heck am I supposed to do after they leave? Start another one? I mean, what else is there for those of us who ride this reason into marriage? I can already tell this is going to be hard for me. The thought of my kids growing up and leaving the house makes me want to cry already. Empty nest typically affects women more than men, but it does affect both genders, and it does affect many of us.

As long as we are talking about our children leaving us, we may as well talk about the tragic deaths of our children that many of us have had to walk through. I cannot imagine and, to be honest, do not even want to think about having to walk through that tragedy. I know that many of you have had to walk through that. I know that because in 2005, 11,358 kids between the ages of one and fourteen died as a result of accidents and of congenital disease in the United States. That is an average of thirty-one kids a day. That is a lot of gut-wrenching tragedy, and I am so sorry for those of you who have suffered this.

I can safely say that I never allowed this possibility to enter my mind while thinking about the family I would raise. If I did I would then have to ask myself if I could survive it. It was a path that I just did not want to go down because if I went there it would shatter my model of the family I was going to be a part of. That was just not acceptable. However, I do not think it is particularly helpful to never think about this possibility. If we walk through life never even considering this could happen, then we also have no strategy to deal with it if it does. I am not talking about strategy like what to do and when to do it in regards to funeral and other arrangements. I am talking about being healed enough to look to God first and stand up to fight the anger, hatred, self-blame, bitterness, and unforgiveness that would be waiting to come in and set up shop. Hopelessness and despair would also be formidable.

I have never lost a child, but I know enough pain to know that those things are just waiting for tragedy to strike so that they can come in and kick you when you are down. It is just the way they operate. I have been a paramedic for years, and thankfully I have only had to deal with losing a child once. That is enough and more than anyone should ever have to deal with or walk through. I felt the parents' pain. I cried with them. None of us could ever begin to understand the pain and suffering that comes with losing a child. All I got was a glimpse, and that was enough for me. I'm not so sure that if we had the opportunity to feel the pain of the tragic loss of a child we would be so eager to get married and have kids. I am not saying that the answer is to never have kids in order to avoid pain; I'm just saying there are things we never consider when we daydream about what it's going to be like to have kids someday.

There is another tough issue that we need to take time to deal with. This was actually a fear of mine because if it happened it would have shattered my family model. It is the possibility of having a child that has Down syndrome, who is autistic, or who has any other mental or developmental problems. I thought about this possibility a handful of times, and it made me wonder what I would do. It hurt me to think about it. We all want normal healthy kids, right? Well, the truth is we don't always get normal, healthy kids.

I have a great friend that I care about deeply who has a baby with Down syndrome. It has been hard on him at times, it has been hard on his wife, and it has been hard on his marriage. I am sure many of you would say the same thing. I will tell you one thing though. That child is a joy and a blessing from God. There is no question that baby is loved by his parents. However, I am sure that there was a process of grieving for both of them. Their family model was shattered, and they had to form a new one. One that involved something that they did not think they would ever have to deal with. According to www.kidshealth. org, one out of every eight hundred babies is born with Down syndrome. That number sounds a lot higher than I would have thought. I know that I would have adapted and loved the child just as much as my other kids, but I also know that there would be a grieving process and I would need God to bring healing to my brokenness.

Not only do we have to deal with our lifelong expectations of what raising a family would be like crashing down around us after the deaths or unexpected conditions of our children, we also must consider the affect these things have on our marriage relationships. According to www.divorce360.com, 16 percent of married couples get divorced after the death of a child. That may not seem like a huge number, but there are things we don't see in this statistic. The 84 percent of couples who are able to remain married have a long and difficult road to healing ahead of them. The emotional pain of loss can take years and years to heal, which, of course, can strain our marriage relationships. There are also other issues that must be dealt with as a result of tragic loss or unexpected conditions. Things like bitterness, blame, unforgiveness, guilt, shame, regret, fear, anxiety, worry, dread, self-bitterness, self-unforgiveness, self-blame, self-hatred, jealousy, and envy begin to take hold of us. If these issues are pushed down instead of dealt with, they will destroy our marriage relationships even if our marriages remain intact. The question looms: If our marriages stayed together but our relationship was destroyed, did we really survive?

As we move on with our discussion about kids, we must talk about all of the "bad" decisions our children seem to make. There is a pattern of thought that says kids become terrible when they are teenagers. We begin to reminisce to the days when little Johnny was perfect. Well, little Johnny has never been perfect. It's just that as he has grown, so have the offenses. If sin is sin in God's eyes and he does not hold one sin as greater than any other sin, then the bad decision that my son made the other day to hit his younger sister would be and is on the same level as one of your teenage kids sneaking out of the house, going to a party, getting drunk or high, having sex for the first time and getting pregnant. Let's just face it.

Our kids are going to make bad decisions. In my perfect model, my kids will wait to have sex until they are married, they will not do drugs, and they will not abuse alcohol. They will also never break the law. Now this is what I pray for, but I cannot trust that these things will happen the way I want them to. Actually, it is a rare thing these days for any of this to happen the way that we would like it to. That is a very unfortunate fact. The hardest thing for me to deal with would be for my little girl to have sex before she got married. That probably reveals some things I need to work out. Maybe I have some expectations on her that I shouldn't have. Actually I probably have expectations on both of my children that I shouldn't have.

I really wanted a boy and a girl. My expectation was that the boy would love sports and be good at them. He would like to play video games and would just be a lot of fun. My girl would be just the sweetest little thing. She would be a "daddy's girl." She would stay sweet and pure until she gets married so that she can be sweet and pure for that guy, whoever he is. She would never be drunk or high. Many of you can relate to those expectations. The problem is that they are expectations, and many of us have been let down by them. Failed expectations translate into our kids letting us down. With that comes disappointment and many times bitterness and self-blame. In reality they have let down expectations that really should not be there.

We have already talked about hope and the best that we can do here is hope that our children will make good choices and live as God would have them live.

Loss of Freedom

So we have kids, and we watch our free time fly out of the window. What comes back in the window is more responsibility and far less time for us. I do not know how I maintained this idea, but in my family model, I was still doing whatever I wanted to do whenever I wanted to do it. Well, I found out real quick that is not reality. We were discussing this in our small group, and one of the members was talking about how she got a phone call from a friend of hers who does not have kids. This friend was going to the mall and then to wherever. She asked if the member of our group wanted to come along. This member of our group has two kids and was "stuck" at home with them, so she could not go. She talked about how she envied her friend a little for her freedom to go wherever whenever.

We all feel like that at times. Is it selfish? Absolutely, but you cannot deny that selfishness can be a part of you and has the ability to make you unhappy with the way things are. So great, we got married so that we could raise a family, and now we are unhappy because we don't have the freedom we had when we did not have a family. Kara and I had our son about ten months after we got married, so we don't even really know what it's like to be a married couple without kids.

* * *

From Kara:

If you are a person who does not yet have children and are reading this thinking, *My children will respect me* or *I will not have issues with my kids because I will know how to properly raise them,* well, it is time for a wake-up call. It is absolutely impossible to judge these things until you yourself are a parent. Before I had kids, I would see a child in the store throwing an absolute fit and the mother would grit her teeth and whisper threats to the child. Sometimes this would work, sometimes this wouldn't, but the thought that would always cross my mind is this: *My child will never act that way in public because I will be a better parent than that mother/father.* Well, guess what? Sometimes my children act like that in the store. I now look at those parents and sympathize with them. Kids are *kids!* They will act out; they *will* test the boundaries no matter how good of a parent you are.

My children are still young so I have yet to know what having teenagers or being an empty-nester will be like, but I pray God gives me the strength to deal properly with these issues because I know that they will come and I know that they will not be easy. It is unfortunate when parents' lives revolve around their children because when they are gone you have nothing left. I believe that this is a form of idol worship. Anytime you place anything or anyone above God, it is idol worship, period. I also firmly believe that your spouse is to come before your children. It is important to have time away from your children for both your marriage and your sanity. If your marriage is falling apart, that will negatively affect your children, but if your marriage is intact and you are truly keeping God at the center, your children will be blessed because of it.

* * *

So let's get this straight. We got married so that we could have and raise a family, and we got pregnancy problems and annoying and disrespectful kids who make bad decisions. We got the possibility of having to walk through the death of a child and the possibility of having a child with mental or developmental problems. We got a 16 percent chance of getting divorced as a result and the 100 percent chance of dealing with many issues in which the primary purpose is to steal, kill, and destroy us. We also lost our freedom and have to deal with lots more responsibility. We have lost the bodies that we used to have forever, and our kids will eventually leave us. Really, I do not need to be married to experience all of this. Yes, there are some rewarding times and joy, but for the most part, what's the point?

?

Because I Have To

I ministered for a couple of years with Operation Light Force, a healing and deliverance ministry. Within the first couple of months of 2008, I met a woman in a ministry appointment who has become a good friend of mine. God has done some wonderful and miraculous things in her life. She has experienced much healing on the physical, emotional, and spiritual levels. Over the course of that year, we talked about many things as God brought revelation and healing.

One of the main things that God did for this woman was to restore her sense of identity. She had lost who she was and is, very possibly, just over the last couple of months really beginning to know who she really is and had always been. The problem was that her identity was wrapped up in a man. Actually, it was wrapped up in a relationship. This woman had found her identity in being married. She believed that the only way she would be someone was for her to be married. So she believed that in order to survive she had to get married.

One of the major problems with this belief is that sometimes we settle just so we can be comfortable. This idea of settling might seem okay at first, but fast forward fifteen years and you will most likely be battling bitterness and resentment against your spouse and more likely yourself. As far as this woman's testimony, God completely tore down that old identity and rebuilt it in him. It was painful, but a remarkable healing occurred. Praise God!

When our identity is wrapped up in the relationship, it puts a lot of pressure on us not to just get married but to stay married. So instead of expressing feelings that may bring conflict, we just keep pressing onward all the while letting the resentment build. If that marriage falls apart and is destroyed, then who are we? We better be able to find someone quick to fill that gap, right?

I remember quite well the pressure to be married. I felt it most of my life. I remember that I did not feel like it was even an option not to get married. I believed that it was normal and that there was something wrong with you if you were not married. There is an image of an old maid with lots of cats in my head, and that is what I equated to not being married. I believed that if you did not get married, you would live a very sad and depressing life and eventually die alone. There is a lot of fear in that belief. So what are the reasons that we feel we have to get married? For this friend of mine, it was an identity issue, but even that has a deeper root. So let's talk about some of them.

Self-Acceptance

This is a big one. This is the one that hits closest to home for me. What does it mean if we are not married? It means that there was no one out of the billions of people on this earth that wanted us enough to marry us, right? Talk about rejection, and we do not handle rejection very well, do we? So we take steps to try to correct the problem. Sometimes it is by changing our personalities, and sometimes it is with surgery to improve our physical appearance. So when those things do not work, what are we left with? We are left with trying to figure out and desperately wanting to know what is wrong with us that we cannot seem to find someone to marry. Then we come to our own conclusions about what is wrong with us. They are usually things like "I guess I am just ugly" or "There is just something wrong with the way I act" or how about this one: "I have just done too many bad things and no good guy is going to want me"? These are judgments that we have made against ourselves, and we believe them so that there is nothing we can do to change our beliefs. We can change the way we look with surgery and change the way we act, but those things do not change the beliefs that we have about ourselves. Those are just outward things, but there is no inward change.

So now we hate ourselves, and when a person comes along who does want to marry us, we can't understand why, so we don't let them in to who we really are. That scheme will play throughout the life of your marriage unless it is exposed and dealt with. See, if you feel lucky that someone wanted to marry you, you will always just be hanging on and not really emotionally attached. The reason is if you get honest with yourself you will find that you really expect, at some point, for your spouse to find someone better than you and leave. Then what happens? Well, you have experienced the ultimate rejection in your eyes, which further solidifies the self-hatred, and to top it off, you are back in the "not married" category. Now you have to deal with the "get married" pressures all over again.

I was talking to a good friend of mine one night, and we were talking about marriage. He told me that if his wife ever found someone that could provide for her better than he could and could make her happier than he could, then he loved her enough to let her go. That sounded honorable to him, and maybe it does to some of you as well. The truth is that statement is full of self-hatred and rejection. It is not that he loves her enough to let her go, but it is that he does not love himself enough to say, "Hey, we are in a rough spot, but you made a promise to stick with me, so do it." He does not believe he is worthy of that. That statement is also rooted in something that we call a bitter root expectation. That is when you expect something bad to happen. These things are not good things to carry around with you. The reason is that it gives Satan a right to put things in position and push them to happen. If this concept is foreign to you, take a moment to reflect back on the bad things you expected to happen that actually ended up happening. I am sure you can come up with a few.

I remember in the first couple of years in my marriage I was really struggling with some addictions. I felt so bad about myself because of what I put my wife through. I told her later on that I would not have blamed her if she would have left during that time period. I have since broken the power of those words, and I do not believe that way anymore. My wife made a covenant with me, and I am worthy of being stood by no matter what I am struggling with. Your spouse has made a covenant to stand by you, and you are worthy of it. Anything that tells you different is a lie.

The point is that just because you get married for self-acceptance does not mean that the self-rejection goes away. We talked about that in an earlier chapter. But why does it seem like you are only normal if you get married? Well, it is probably because most of us get married. From the resources I pulled, I gathered that somewhere between 5 *and* 30 *percent* of us never get married. Either way you look at it, you are in the minority if you do not get married. That means you are different according to the statistics. Is that okay with you? Some have chosen a life of singleness, but most of us are looking for that person we can spend the rest of our lives with.

With every breakup comes more rejection, and with every

helping of rejection comes more self-hate, and with every helping of self-hate comes despair and hopelessness and the lies that you are alone now and you will always be that way. So we not only want to, but we feel like and believe that we have to get married so that we can accept ourselves. So we get married, and the self-acceptance that we thought we would gain just does not seem to materialize. What's the point?

Social Acceptance

I used to love to do things by myself. As I have walked through much healing, some of that desire has been taken away. I have found that as I love myself more and more, I want to have people around me, mainly my wife, Kara. I used to love going to the movies by myself. I would get an empty chair on either side and just relax and fan out. I would not have to share my popcorn or soda with anyone. I would not have to worry about Kara asking me, "What's going on?" forty-five minutes into the movie and then expect a full synopsis for the last forty-five minutes. It was just fun to me. It was comfortable. I do believe that some of that comfort came from not having to expose my emotion to anyone I knew. That is unhealthy, and God has brought some healing and continues to bring healing to that area for me. I am not saying that it is wrong to go to see a movie by yourself, but what I am saying is check your motives.

I have expressed this whole thing to my wife at times about how I enjoy going to the movies alone. She would just tell me that I am weird. She would ask me if I was embarrassed to be there by myself. The truth is that sometimes I would look around and see couples and get a little uncomfortable, but I would just shake it off and watch the movie. Now my wife was, before God took her through some healing, at the other extreme where she did not like to do and was even uncomfortable doing anything by herself. There was absolutely no way she could understand why I would want to do something like that.

We have both since moved a lot closer to that middle ground now where she is comfortable by herself and I am a lot more likely not to do things by myself.

From what I have watched and from my experience, society will tell you that if you go to the movies alone you are a loser and if you have someone to go with you are a winner. That does not just apply to the movies but for most events. According to society, it looks much better for you to show up with someone than to show up with no one. No one wants to be a loser, right? We all want to be liked and for people to think that we are someone special. Men, if we can show up somewhere with a beautiful woman on our arm, then bonus, right? Women, if you can show up somewhere with a strong, successful, and good-looking man, then bonus for you, right?

Then there are the events that you will only be invited to if you are married or involved with someone. We would hate to be left out of that, right? Is it okay with you to show up to church alone? Oh, you want to talk about uncomfortable, how about going to a restaurant and eating a meal by yourself? I have seen it, and I give credit to those of you who are comfortable doing that. I will go see a movie by myself, but I do not think I would go to a restaurant alone.

So what is the best way to make sure that you will always have someone to accompany you places? Let's get married, folks. All you have to do is get married, and you will never have to go to the movies alone. You will never have to go to church alone, and you will always have someone to show up with at parties and events. It is so simple and easy. Get married, and it will all be great. Except married people still go to movies alone, still go to church alone, and often cannot stand the sight of each other enough to show up to parties and events together. However, for those of us who would suck it up and continue to go to all these events together, I have this to say. If the fraction of a percentage worth of time you spend in your life going to events that would make you acceptable by being married is enough for you to overshadow the 99.999999 percent of the time you are not going to events and you can find happiness and fulfillment in that small fraction, then more power to you. However, for those of us that would say that small fraction is not enough, who incidentally are the only ones telling the truth, what's the point of getting married for social acceptance? I mean really, when the party is over or you get back from the movies or whatever event you went to, you walk right back into the same relationship with many issues all with deeper roots.

What other things is society telling you to do that you are failing in? Take a minute and consider that. I do not have to tell you what those things are. Each of us is pressured by different issues. Society tells us that we should do lots of things that many of us just cannot seem to do. So if marriage is all you have, are you really acceptable to society? I should say, do you believe that you are acceptable to society if all you have is a small piece of the pie?

Family Acceptance

Have you seen the movie *Because I Said So?* It is a really cute movie. It is considered a chic-flick, and my wife made me watch it. That is my story anyway. The lead character is played by Mandy Moore, and she is under constant pressure from her mother throughout the movie to meet someone and get married. Do you or did you ever feel pressured by your family to get married? How about when your sibling got married? How did that make you feel? If you are not married, do you feel acceptance from your family or disapproval? If you are married now, think back to before you were married and answer that question. We all want so desperately to have to approval of our parents. I have seen in ministry that those who never seem to have gotten that approval want it so badly, and if they cannot get it from their parents, they try to get it from other places, ironically to try to impress their parents.

I was modeled the "grow up and get married" plan. I do not ever remember my parents saying that it would be okay if I did not get married. That is not their fault. I do not know why they would have felt the need to say that. I felt a lot of pressure from my family to get married. Not by what was said but by what was modeled. Actually, now that I think back, I can remember that it was important to my mother that we kids be in relationships and find someone to marry. It was a desire motivated by self-ishness on her part because it made her feel good about herself if she knew that her kids were desired and were married. She would admit this, and she is not that way anymore. God has taken her through a lot of healing as well. So I guess the pressure that came at me was a mixture of what was said and what was modeled. That pressure increased when my older sister got married. Do we feel rejected by our parents when we are not married? How about when there is divorce? How has your relationship changed with your family because of divorce, if at all?

So we get married and stay married, and everything is okay now between us and our families, right? I want to bring back the truth about perception and reality at this point. Many times we perceive rejection when in reality no one is rejecting us at all. I may have perceived that if I did not get married my parents would reject me, but I know that not to be true. That is not reality. The lie of rejection was real and strong but not truth.

Other times a very wounded and broken parent will tell a child that if they do not get married they are worthless. That is very painful, but it happens. Now if that child does not get married and the parent rejects them, that rejection is not just perception, but it is reality. Either way it feels the same. It does not matter if it is just perception or reality; the feelings are the same.

So let's say that each of these people in the different scenarios does get married. To those of you who fit that description, I have this to say: chances are that if being married makes you acceptable to your family, whether it be perception or reality based, then there are plenty of other things that you feel you need to do to gain that acceptance from them, and being married only matters a small bit. What else do you believe that you need to do to gain your family's acceptance? Furthermore, is it really even worth it? Should you have to work that hard for approval?

So you got married in order to get the approval of your family. Now, on top of realizing that was not enough to get what you were after, you have to deal with all the struggles that a married couple faces. Are you up for that? Maybe you do feel like getting married got you the approval that you were after from your family. Good for you. However, you must now realize that your family's approval is hinging on assumption that your marriage is going to go the distance. Well, you only have a 50 *to* 60 *percent* chance of that happening. What would your family think of a divorce? Chances are that they will be even more disappointed in you than before. That is a lot of pressure, so you better not do anything to rock the boat with your spouse. That means suppressing a lot of things that can make for a pretty miserable life. I know many of you can relate to this. I have seen it in ministry and experienced it in my own marriage. So, really, come on. Getting married for the approval of your family? What's the point?

So now we wrap this whole reason "because I have to" up. Some of you got married for self-acceptance and found that you feel the same about yourself after you getting married as you did before you got married. Some of us got married so that society would accept us and found out that while having someone to go to events with looks good, there is an emptiness that we do not know quite how to fill. We have also realized that there is so much more that society requires to be accepted than just being married, and the possibility of us attaining all of those things is slim. Some of us are so desperate for our family's approval that we thought getting married would make us acceptable to them. We have realized that if we don't feel like we have our parents' approval before getting married then we probably don't feel like we have it now. We have also recognized that if we have gained our family's approval by getting married, there is incredible pressure to keep our marriages together.

Do you see the problem here? It does not matter if you got married for self-acceptance, social acceptance, or to be accepted by your family, all three categories are unable to produce the results that we were looking for. This is very evident in my own life. I felt like I had to get married for self-acceptance and to be accepted by my family. As I reflect over the years, I have to admit that I did not gain any self-acceptance, and I am in the category of being pressured to keep my marriage together. I would have an issue with telling my family that I got a divorce. I would feel that maybe I let them down and then they would reject me. I know that is a lie, but it is an attack from the enemy, and the attack is real. So what's the point of getting married at all?

Love

Ah yes. Love. We come to the final reason we are going to discuss. Out of all the reasons, this sounds like the safest, right? This is rock solid. You have to have love in your marriage relationship, right? I could not possibly dismantle this reason, could I? This is the reason to get married that was most repeated back to me. "You fall in love and then get married."

As we move through this chapter, we are not going to dismantle the fact that love needs to be a part of a marriage covenant relationship, but we are in a way. There is a dramatic difference in what we perceive love to be and what it actually is according to God. The strange thing is that even we as Christians have a skewed perception of what love is. Few of us actually understand it. I am not saying that I am one of those few, but I am closer than where I started by the grace of God.

The problem is that as our perception goes, so goes our idea of reality. So if we have a messed up perception of what love is, our idea of the reality of love is also messed up. My understanding of love now is nowhere close to what my understanding of it was years ago. Guess what. I did not get greater understanding because of what my wife and I have been through either. My understanding of love grew as my understanding of God grew.

Let me start out by asking you a question. What is love? It's a hard question, I know, but I want you to take a moment and think about it. I also don't want you to give the correct Bible answer. I have found most of the time what we know intellectually is not what we really believe to be true. **What we really believe is evident in the way we live our lives and how we respond to situations**. What do you believe love is? I will give you an example of what I mean from my own experience.

I have already shared that I was emotionally shut down for eight years and for four years of my marriage. As God brought me through significant healing, I began to see the roots of the bondage. Of course it was because I was afraid of feeling, but why was that?

All throughout my high school and much of my college life, I developed feelings for girls who already had boyfriends. I could not help it. The girls were pretty and fun, so I liked them. Unfortunately, I am not the only one who likes those qualities (go figure), and I seemed to always be one step behind. Well, it felt to me like rejection when they would not dump their current boyfriend for me. I never gave them an ultimatum or anything, but it would just not happen, and I was always crushed.

Now fast forward ten or so years later, and I am in a ministry session for myself discussing belief systems. We were talking about God's love and what that meant to me. I gave them the correct answer according to the Bible, but as things moved ahead, God began to reveal some very interesting beliefs in me. Because of the way that I had been hurt not just by those girls in high school and college but also my own family and others, I had developed the belief that love is pain. No wonder why I shut down emotionally. Who wants to feel pain, and that is what I believed love was. See, I could give the "correct" answer, but that is not what I really believed. Here is a quote from Woody Allen that describes my old belief perfectly:

> To love is to suffer. To avoid suffering one must not love. But then one suffers from not loving. Therefore to love is to suffer, not to love is to suffer. To suffer is to suffer. To be happy is to love. To be happy then is to suffer. But suffering makes one unhappy. Therefore, to be unhappy one must love, or love to suffer, or suffer from too much happiness. I hope you're getting this down.

There is at least one other person out there that has the same belief system about love that I had. Thanks, Woody. This belief system for love also fits perfectly with the reality that the reason "someone to love" was last in my priority list.

I asked my wife what she believed love was. She told me "God." After I gave her a gold star, I read her the previous part where I told you all I do not want you to give the correct biblical answer but to really think about it. She told me "happily ever after." That is better. Love is happily ever after, right? So as long as you are in love, you will be happy forever and exempt from negative things, right? So based on the two answers Kara and I gave, it would be accurate to say we believed love was a feeling or emotion. I believed love was pain, and Kara believed love was happiness. So what other beliefs do we have about love? Here are some quotes:

> There is only one happiness in life—to love and to be loved.
>
> George Sand

> What I needed most was to love and to be loved, eager to be caught. Happily I wrapped those painful bonds around me; and sure enough, I would be lashed with the red hot pokers of jealousy, by suspicions and fear, by burst of anger and quarrels.
>
> St. Augustine

When you are in love you can't fall asleep because reality is better than your dreams.

> Dr. Seuss

Women wished to be loved not because they are pretty, or good, or well bred, or graceful, or intelligent, but because they are themselves.

> Henri Frederic Amiel

The best thing about me is you.

> Shannon Crown

Pleasure of love lasts but a moment, pain of love lasts a lifetime.

> Bette Davis

If you love me, let me know. If not, please gently let me go.

> Anonymous

You come to love not by finding the perfect person, but by seeing an imperfect person perfectly.

> Sam Keen

To the world you may be one person, but to one person you may be the world.

> Heather Cortez

The best and most beautiful things in the world cannot be seen or even touched. They must be felt with the heart.

> Helen Keller

All of these quotes were taken from the top ten best love quotes of all time. So if these quotes were judged by people to be put in the top ten, chances are that we all can relate to at least one of them. Here are some quotes taken off a Web blog:

> I have so many "opinions" on love ... but mine is from a different perspective ... (not too much of a romantic). I don't know whether I believe in love at first sight, I think it is

> something that grows over time gradually as you get to know a person more and more, like unwrapping a present. Love, to me, is utter *commitment*.

This person says love is a commitment. So then what happens when the commitment is broken?

> I think love can be defined as something that makes the heart stir, that can't always be explainable, that makes you feel as though you would and could do anything for that other person. Love helps you to "miss" the bad qualities in your lover and makes you happy just because! "Love is a constellation of emotions and experiences related to a sense of strong affection or profound oneness" is one "technical" definition given! Sounds good to me.

So from this quote love hides the bad qualities in our lovers. Trust me, that does not mean they disappear. So then what happens to this person's belief when his lover's bad qualities are exposed and he is crushed by the consequences of that?

I am sure I could go on and on with the quotes and opinions. There is a common problem with all of these quotes and beliefs. The problem is that they make love something that can end abruptly. Just like a feeling or emotion. In the above quotes, we have love ending when commitment is broken, bad qualities are exposed and cause pain, when we love characteristics instead of the person, and when happiness ends. We also have my example and then some quotes about love being pain and suffering. These, along with some others I am sure, are our beliefs of what love is. Our beliefs are skewed, and that is why the reason "because I love him or her" is not good enough to get married.

Our true beliefs of love are skewed because of all the hurts, pains, wounds, and ungodly beliefs we have experienced in relationships that meant, or mean, the most to us. These strongholds make it impossible for us to understand, in our spirits and souls, what love really is according to God. So impossible in fact that unless we first are willing to admit we don't truly understand love and second call upon the only source of perfect love (Father God) to transform our understanding, the perfect love of God will never make it past our intellectual minds, and we will spend our whole lives trying to fill a void.

So let's move on to the next question that I want to ask you. I have seen many headlines in magazines and newspapers about "how you keep your love strong." What do you believe you have to do to keep love strong in your marriage or relationships? What have you tried? What do you want to try? Are you just so tired of trying that you have just given up? It is exhausting trying to keep love in a marriage, isn't it?

Men, do you believe you have to buy your wife gifts so that she knows you love her? Women, do you need to receive gifts from your husband to know that he loves you? Do you help around the house or do outside chores so that your spouse knows that you love him/her? You may say, "Well, if I don't do those things, how will my spouse know that I love him/her?" That is exactly the problem, because the pressure to do enough to maintain that is incredible and is never enough to have security. That was the belief that I fell into.

You may also say, "I do those things because I love him/her." That is a great place to be and we should all be there, but I question how many people who say that actually believe it. That is the "correct" answer, but like I said before, we seldom believe what we know intellectually. For example, underneath that "correct" answer might be insecurity that says, "If I do these things, then he/she will be happier and not leave me." Oftentimes we do those things because we believe it earns us points, and as long as we have positive points, our spouses will not leave us or stray. Why would they leave or cheat if we are doing things to make them happy, right? So our acts of service become motivated by fear. That fear comes from the belief that you alone are just not enough to keep them happy, so we must do things to make them happy. That was my belief, and it is not a great way to live in a relationship.

Here are some other ideas I found to keep your love strong. Have a date every week, snuggle, play games together, write love letters or notes, and remember to say I love you. These are all good ideas, but the problem is people can use those things to gauge how strong their love is, and if those things are not happening, where does love go? And let's not kid ourselves. How long can you really keep those things up on a regular basis? Let's ask ourselves these questions. What are we doing to keep our love strong, and is it working the way we want it to? The problem with doing things to keep love strong is that we are attaching love to acts. We believe love is acts. When the acts stop or are not just happening enough in your opinion, it means love has left your relationship, right? If you believe love is acts, that is the logical conclusion you have to accept. It is impossible for *us* to keep the love strong in our relationships simply by doing things couples are supposed to do with and for each other.

How do you know that your spouse still loves you? During the majority of my marriage, I did not want to think about this question. In my brokenness I would replace that question with "Why does she love me?" Seriously, I asked myself that question a couple of times, and I almost asked her that once. I tried not to think about it very much because it made me feel so bad about myself, but it was there. How did I know Kara still loved me? Forget that question. I didn't even know why she loved me in the first place. I bet I'm not the only one who felt or feels like that. Most of us would answer that question with a phrase starting like this: "Because he/she does ... " Once again we are back to love is acts.

Some time ago, I had an interesting appointment with a woman. I had been ministering to this particular woman for a couple of months, and it didn't seem like we were getting anywhere. The underlying cause of every single one of this woman's problems was she, like most of us, had absolutely no understanding of God's perfect love. She understood it intellectually, but it wasn't real to her. I felt I had tried everything I could to get her to see she was trying to fill her love tank from empty sources. Finally, I looked at her and said, "Does God love you?" She said, "Yes, of course he does." I asked her, "How do you know?" She looked at me in silence, completely baffled with fear in her eyes. She had no answer. I asked her, "Do your children love you?" She said, "Yes." I asked her, "How do you know?" She said, "Because they respect and help me." I asked her, "Does your husband love you?" Through tears she said, "No." I asked her softly, "How do you know?" She answered, "Because he doesn't respect me and never does anything for me."

This woman had some pretty heavy things happening in her life. Her marriage was crashing down around her as well as her health. Nothing was what she wanted it to be. What she needed most was the perfect love of God to flood her entire being, but her belief that love is acts kept her trapped in the lie she's not loved. Her kids did not respect and help her all of the time, so her love was inconsistent there; she accepted the perception her husband didn't love her anymore; and, most importantly, she couldn't point to anything God had done for her recently to show her how much he loves her. Her whole world was falling apart, and she was alone and unloved. At the root of it all was a lack of revelation and understanding of God's perfect love, and that lack had defiled every relationship she ever had.

Here is a little reality. Ninety-nine percent of the time there are no acts going on, so how do you know that your spouse still loves you? Are you afraid of that question? Are you afraid you might have to say "I don't know" and the implications of admitting that? You might say, "I know my spouse loves me because he/she tells me." Ask yourself how many times you need to hear those words from your spouse to live in the security that he/she still loves you. Then ask yourself if that number is reached every day. Acts fail, words fail, and anything else we try to do always carries with it the possibility that it will fail. So what is the conclusion? The conclusion is that the majority of us live through our marriages never really knowing whether or not our spouses still love us.

Can love grow? I used to think so. I don't think that way anymore. What I think now is that our understanding of love grows by revelation from God as we allow God to heal and set us free. If love can grow in our relationships, that means we are responsible for doing the tasks to make it grow, right? So what are you doing to make your love grow? We might point back to all of the things we do to keep love strong. However, if those things fail in those arenas, we cannot use them here either.

So what, you get one dose of love and that is it? Well, sort of. If you never let God teach you what love really is, then it will stay small. That is the way most of us live in our relationships. We do not really understand love, so we treat it as something that needs to be maintained; and if we cannot maintain it, then it is disposable. Also, as long as we do not understand love, it will always be just a feeling to us and nothing more.

The picture I get is of God setting a table before us. On that table, God has placed every fruit of his spirit, and he is looking to us saying, "Come and get it." A lot of times we ask God for more peace. We ask for more love. In our prayer time and in our times of distress, we ask for more of every fruit of the Holy Spirit. Does God see our need for peace and only give us a small "helping"? Is that your impression of a loving God? What would it look like if the full measure of peace has already been given and it's up to us to come and get it? What if we began to pray for understanding of that perfect peace Isaiah talks about instead of for more peace? What if we began to pray for more understanding of God's love instead of more of God's love? When someone comes into salvation, the full measure of every single fruit of the Holy Spirit is made available to him or her, and at that point, it becomes a journey of revelation and understanding. I heard someone say this jewel of wisdom: "We cannot do God's part, and God will not do our part." It's a relationship that God wants.

So you believe that your spouse loves you. What about betrayal, lies, and deception? We already talked about how there is an 80 percent chance that there will be unfaithfulness at some point throughout your marriage. Where does love fit into that? Many of us would say if your spouse cheats on you then he/she does not really love you. You don't hurt someone you love like that, right? Well, if that is true, then love fails 80 percent of the time in our marriages. That is pretty staggering. That also says that we believe love is just a feeling we can fall out of. But that would never happen in your marriage, right? Your love is different. Your love is better than 80 percent of relationships? Congratulations.

Can you fall out of love? I used to say yes, and that scared me. My answer is now "I hope not." If it is possible to fall out of love, then what does that say for our relationship with God? Can God fall out of love with us? Many Christians would give the correct answer here and say a person cannot fall out of love. I would say that if we really believe love is nothing more than a feeling or emotion, we would have to say that it is possible, in fact, to fall out of love.

We just discovered that most of us walk through our marriages not really knowing if our spouses still love us. However, I am sure there was a particular point you did know that your spouse loved you. So if he/she loved you at one point but you don't know if he/she does now, you would say that it must be possible to fall out of love. I would say that according to what most of us truly believe love is, it is very possible to fall out of love.

I found a quiz on the Internet that you can take to see if you are falling out of love. You hear that reason in the movies and on TV, and maybe you have even said it. You may be in a marriage right now and have said, "I just don't love him/her anymore." But what does that do to your understanding of what love is?

I thought love never fails. That's what the Bible says in 1

Corinthians 13:8. However, many of you are coming with a different perspective. You have seen love fail time and time again. It has failed you or someone you care about. If someone can fall out of love, that means love can fail. That is very disturbing because many of us put our hope and trust in love. Many of us believe that to fall in love makes our lives significant. So if love can fail, then how much hope do you have? How much do you think your life matters?

. . .

From Kara:

We have all heard the song "All You Need is Love." This statement is actually a true statement, except that I don't believe this song is referring to the love of God. I sought love in any possible place that I could find it. I sought validation from family, friends, and most prominently, the opposite sex.

When I married Jesse, I was so excited. I had finally found the key to happiness, or so I thought. I was under the impression that, because I was getting married, I would always feel and experience the depths of love. I was not equating in any way the love of and from God to my relationship with Jesse. Of course I said that God was the center of our marriage, but I didn't really know what that meant. The love that I gave to and received from Jesse was shallow. Because I had built my thoughts of love around relationships with humans, I was left feeling empty and needing something or someone to constantly fill that void. It wasn't until I filled my "love void" with God that I was able to have and receive true agape love.

. . .

So we get married for someone to love, right? Okay then, we got married for something we don't really understand. We also have no power to make it grow on our own and get very tired trying. We have no idea if our spouses really love us, and we have no idea how to keep them loving us. Now enter in betrayal, lies, and deception, and we see, according to our perspective, 80 percent of love failing. We have also come to realize we really believe it's possible to fall out of love. So I ask you, what's the point of getting married?

Part A Wrap-up

I am glad that it is time to bring Part A to a close. I am tired of writing negativity. It is time to instill some hope in you all. For myself too. I need some hope after writing that.

The thing is that some of the reasons I talked about are not necessarily wrong, and I believe that many of them do have a place. However, there is a block inside most of us that is preventing us from attainting the godliness that was supposed to accompany these reasons. I know that there was definitely a block in me, and that block is still being healed every day as I walk with the Lord. Most of the reasons that I talked about were meant to supplement the real purpose of marriage in order to bring us more insight into who God is and to give us pleasure. The mistake that we have made is to use these reasons as the main force driving us to get married and we supplement them with God. I shouldn't have to tell you that it doesn't work that way.

The main thing I want to do in the pages ahead is to reveal what I believe to be the ultimate purpose of marriage and to then give you a strategy to attain that purpose, and the strategy may surprise you. It is not your normal everyday strategy.

I want to share something personal at this point because it may tie together some loose ends. Pay close attention to what follows because this is a little uncomfortable, and I think this could speak to many of you and especially those of you that have not been married yet. As I look back over all the reasons that we get married, I can point to "someone to build a family with," "because I have to," and "because I love her" as my reasons for getting married. However, as I reflect back to some feelings that I remember having as we were dating and engaged, the order I would put those reasons in may surprise you. The order is:

1. Because I have to

2. Someone to build a family with

3. Because I love her

That sounds a little disturbing, but I was a wounded person; and in those first two reasons, there is a lot of fear. Fear is very strong in my generational line, and it was very strong in me. Looking back, it makes sense that I would worry about and take care of first what might bring me peace of mind. Now I praise God and give him the glory because I did not settle. I married exactly the person that God had for me. I ended up marrying the first person that I ever really seriously dated. I believe that God knew that my woundedness would make me want to just settle, so he brought the woman he had for me at just the right time. I am now convinced that because of my brokenness and the fear that was in me that if God did not bring Kara when he did I would have settled for someone less than what God had planned for me.

* * *

From Kara:

As a young child, I dreamed of being a wife and a mother. I was, like many little girls, constantly playing house and being a mommy to my many dolls. Unlike many other children, this was *all* that I wanted to be when I grew up. I never had dreams of being a teacher, doctor, nurse, veterinarian, or any of the various other occupations that my childhood friends spoke of. I simply never had any career ambition and to be quite honest still don't.

When playing house, I fell in love with the idea of always having someone around. Even as a child, I can remember being terrified of the thought of being alone. Fear was *huge* for me. My primary three reasons for getting married were:

1. Someone to share our lives and intimacy with

2. Someone to build a family with

3. Because I love him/her

Because of my fear of being alone, I had a strong desire in me to marry young. I figured the sooner I got married the better. Being married guaranteed that I would never be lonely, or so I thought. When I began to have feelings of loneliness, my world began to crumble around me. I had built my life around the idea that my spouse would complete me and be everything that I ever needed. I cannot even begin to list the many things that are wrong with this mind-set. The main problem with this idea is that my identity was wrapped up in my spouse and not the fact that I was a child of God.

* * *

As you all reflect on this, you very well may realize that the reasons that you got married pushed you to settle for less than what God had for you. Those of you who are not married, be aware these reasons will try to push you into a relationship that God has not intended for you to be in. My prayer is that God will use our experience to prevent any of you from falling into that trap. In Part B we will discuss what God's intention for marriage really is and what to line up your current marriage or relationship with.

However, before we move on I feel like it's very important that we spend just a little bit of time discussing something that has the power to (and very often does) ruin everything. It is the essential issue that must be dealt with if we want any hope of freedom. It is the mortar holding all bondage together and most of the time we don't even know it's there. I'm talking about Pride. Pride is the foundation of the home our enemy builds in us. It holds everything evil and ungodly up. If the enemy wants to enslave us he must first lay the foundation of Pride. Therefore, if we want the house the enemy has built to crumple we must first strip away the foundation of Pride and replace it with a foundation of Humility. The house of the enemy cannot stand on Humility.

Pride is so dangerous because of this:

The pride of your heart has deceived you, you who live in the clefts of the rocks and make your home on the heights, you who say to yourself, "Who can bring me down to the ground?"

Obadiah 1:3 (NIV)

Pride is the only spirit mentioned in the Bible that has the ability to deceive our hearts. Pride will blind us to our own captivity making us believe that we are free when we are really in bondage. That is why someone else's honest assessment of us is valuable. Many times self-evaluation is hard because there are things we can't see.

Pride may have been a factor as you have read this book. You may have been thinking about how good this book would be for someone else as you read. Pride will always deflect you away from truly evaluating yourself and focus your mind on evaluating others. Below I have listed some of the "fruits of Pride" for you to take a look at. Please take the time to check the ones that apply to you. When you are through the list I encourage you to repent and ask God to forgive you for the Pride in your heart. After that tell that spirit of Pride to leave you in the name of Jesus and ask the Holy Spirit to fill you with humility and to open your eyes to see the truth! I believe this is essential before you move on. The journey to transformation and freedom begins with humility.

1. I tend to be *self-sufficient* in the way I live my life. I don't live with a constant awareness that my every breath is dependent upon the will of God. I tend to think I have enough strength, ability, and wisdom to live and manage my life. My practice of the spiritual disciplines is inconsistent and superficial. I don't like to ask others for help. (See 2 Cor. 3:5)

2. I am often *anxious* about my life and the future. I tend not to trust God and rarely experience His abiding and transcendent peace in my soul. I have a hard time sleeping at night because of fearful thoughts and burdens I carry.

3. I am overly *self-conscious*. I tend to replay in my mind how I did, what I said, how I am coming across to others, etc. I am very concerned about what people think of me. I think about these things constantly.

4. I *fear man* more than God. I am afraid of others and make decisions about what I will say or do based upon this fear. I am afraid to take a stand for things that are right. I am concerned with how people will react to me

or perceive my actions or words. I don't often think about God's opinion in a matter and rarely think there could be consequences for disobeying him. I primarily seek the approval of man and not of God.

5. I often feel *insecure.* I don't want to try new things or step out into uncomfortable situations because I'm afraid I'll fail or look foolish. I am easily embarrassed.

6. I regularly *compare myself* to others. I am performance oriented. I feel that I have greater worth if I do well.

7. I am *self-critical.* I tend to be a perfectionist. I can't stand for little things to be wrong because they reflect poorly on me. I have a hard time putting my mistakes behind me.

8. I *desire to receive credit and recognition* for what I do. I like people to see what I do and let me know that they noticed. I feel hurt or offended when they don't. I am overly concerned about my reputation and hate being misunderstood.

9. I want people to be *impressed with me.* I like to make my accomplishments known.

10. I tend to be *deceptive* about myself. I find myself lying to preserve my reputation. I find myself hiding the truth about myself, especially about sins, weaknesses, etc. I don't want people to know who I really am.

11. I am *selfishly ambitious.* I really want to get ahead. I like having a position or title. I far prefer leading to following.

12. I am *overly competitive.* I always want to win or come out on top and it bothers me when I don't.

13. I like to be the *center of attention* and will say or do things to draw attention to myself.

14. I *like to talk, especially about myself* or persons or things I am involved with. I want people to know what I am doing or thinking. I would rather speak than listen.

15. I am *self-serving*. When asked to do something, I find myself asking, "How will doing this help me, or will I be inconvenienced?"

16. I am *not very excited about seeing or making others successful*. I tend to feel envious, jealous, or critical towards those who are doing well or being honored.

17. I *feel special or superior* because of what I have or do.

18. I *think highly of myself*. In relation to others I typically see myself as more mature and more gifted. In most situations, I have more to offer than others even though I may not say so. I don't consider myself average or ordinary.

19. I tend to *give myself credit* for who I am and what I accomplish. I only occasionally think about or recognize that all that I am or have comes from God.

20. I tend to be *self-righteous*. I can think that I really have something to offer God. I would never say so, but I think God did well to save me. I seldom think about or recognize my utter depravity and helplessness apart from God.

21. I *feel deserving*. I think I deserve what I have. In fact, I think I ought to have more, considering how well I have lived or in light of all I have done.

22. I often feel *ungrateful*. I tend to grumble about what I have or my lot in life.

23. I find myself wallowing in *self-pity*. I am consumed with how I am treated by God and others. I tend to feel mistreated or misunderstood. I seldom recognize or sympathize with what's going on with others around me because I feel that I have it worse than they do.

24. I can be *jealous or envious* of other's abilities, possessions, positions, or accomplishments. Want to be what others are or want to have what others have. Pride makes us envious of what others have, think we should have it, or deserve it. I find it hard to rejoice with others when they are blessed by God.

25. I am pretty *insensitive* to others. I feel that some people just aren't worth caring about.

26. I have a *know-it-all attitude*. I am impressed by my own knowledge. I feel like there isn't much I can learn from other people, especially those less mature than me.

27. I have a *hard time listening to ordinary people*. I listen better to those I respect or people I am wanting to leave with a good impression. I don't honestly listen when someone else is speaking because I am usually planning what I am going to say next.

28. I *like to reveal my own mind*. I have an answer for practically every situation. I feel compelled to balance everyone else out.

29. I *interrupt people* regularly. I don't let people finish what they are saying.

30. I *feel compelled to stop people* when they start to share something with me I already know.

31. I find it *hard to admit it when I don't know something.* When someone asks me something I don't know, I will make up an answer rather than admit I don't know.

32. I *listen to teaching with other people in mind.* I constantly think of those folks who need to hear this teaching and wish they were here.

33. I'm *not very open to input.* I don't pursue correction for my own life. I tend to be unteachable and slow to repent when corrected. I don't really see correction as a positive thing. I am offended when people probe the motivations of my heart or seek to adjust me.

34. I have a *hard time admitting that I am wrong.* I find myself covering up or excusing my sins. It is hard for me to confess my sins to others or to ask for forgiveness.

35. I *resent people* who attempt to correct me. I don't respond with gratefulness and sincere appreciation for their input. Instead I am tempted to accuse them and dwell on their faults. I get bitter and withdraw.

36. I am *easily angered and offended.* I don't like being crossed or disagreed with. I find myself thinking, "I can't believe they did that to me." I often feel wronged.

37. I have *"personality conflicts"* with others. I have a hard time getting along with certain kinds of people.

38. I *lack respect* for other people. I don't think very highly of most people. I have a hard time encouraging and honoring others unless they really do something great.

39. I am a *slanderer.* I find myself either giving or receiving evil reports about others. Often times the things I say or hear are true about other people. I am not concerned about the effect of slander on me because of my maturity level. I think I can handle it. I only share with others the things I really think they need to know. I don't tell all.

40. I am *divisive.* I tend to resist or resent authority. I don't like other people to give me orders or directions.

41. I like to *demean or put others down.* At times, people need to be adjusted and put in their place. This includes leaders. Other people need to be humble and have a "sober" assessment of themselves.

42. I tend to be *critical of others.* I find myself feeling or talking negatively about people. I subtly feel better about myself when I see how bad someone else is.

43. I am *self-willed and stubborn.* I have a hard time cooperating with others. I really prefer my own way and often insist on getting it.

44. I am *independent and uncommitted.* I don't really see why I need other people. I can easily separate myself from others. I don't get much out of the small group meetings.

45. I am *unaccountable.* I don't ask others to hold me responsible to follow through on my commitments. I don't really need accountability for my words and actions.

46. I am *unsubmissive.* I don't like being under the authority of another person. I don't see submission as a good and necessary provision from God for my life. I have a hard time supporting and serving those over me. I don't "look up" to people and I like to be in charge. Other people may need leaders, but I don't. It is important that my voice is heard.

47. I really appreciate somebody taking the time to put this paper together. It will really be a big help to my friends and family. However, I don't really need this because *I think I'm pretty humble already.*

?

Marriage: What's the Point?

So now that we have dismantled all of our reasons for getting married, we have to be left wondering what the point of marriage really is.

Let's go back to that horrible Wednesday night I talked about in the beginning. I said it wasn't until that point that I really understood I wasn't the same person I used to be. Let me explain.

As I looked at my broken wife, I was overcome with compassion. That was definitely God-given, and I praise him for that. As he filled me with compassion, I decided I was ready to listen to him. God told me to open my arms and embrace my wife. Even though God was filling me with compassion, it took every ounce of my strength to open my arms to her. I thought I wouldn't be able to do it, but then God gave me even more of his strength and resolve. So I opened my arms, and it was at that moment that God put us on the fast track to healing from this devastating event. It was at that point that I told her that I chose to forgive her. Kara looked up at me in disbelief. She was shocked by what I had said. She couldn't understand why I would forgive her. She told me that she would do anything that I wanted to do. She would do anything I asked. I looked at her a moment as God gave me another dose of the Holy Spirit, and I said, "I want you to forgive yourself." Kara would later tell me she had never really understood the grace of God until that moment. Now I truly believe that I, in and of myself, would not have been able to come up with that response, so I know that was God. My response in this situation was a direct testimony of the healing God worked in me over the year prior to this tragedy. God had ripped off layers of self-hatred, unforgiveness, religion, and much more. God, in his astounding grace, had given me the tools I needed to deal with something like this. The only question was whether or not I was going to use them. There was a dark and intense battle for my soul that night. I shudder when I think about the different ways it could have gone.

I did leave that night and went to my parents' house. They were up when I got there, and we talked for a while. The next day I went home, and my parents took the kids for the weekend. The next couple of days were a mixture of unbelievable pain and miraculous healing. The months that followed were just as interesting.

Kara has walked and is walking through healing and has become a totally different person. The scheme from the enemy that she fell for was exposed, and she now knows why it was easy for her to fall. Kara and I are not the same people we used to be. Not by a long shot. Our relationship is not the same that it once was. Praise God for that! This may sound too good to be true, but our marriage is so much better than it once was. We are both healed and being healed and continue to be made whole. It has been amazing. The professionals claim it takes at least two years to just get past the grief. Glory to God that he does not work for those people. I am not going to take the time to list everything that God has done for us since that Wednesday night, but suffice it to say there is much to list.

As we continue to talk about different issues, I will share what God has taught us through this tragedy. I am not saying that it has been an easy road by any means. There were numerous times when I was so down I did not think I could live anymore. I have been to the depths and it's an ugly place. There were lots of times I felt I wanted to just leave her and a couple times I almost walked out of the door. I carried around so much heaviness. There were so many tears and indescribable heartache.

God has restored my marriage. God has worked a miracle. The miracle is that we are still together and that we have a more intimate relationship than we have ever had. Listen, I am not going to pretend as if I don't ever hurt anymore. We are one and a half years past this tragedy. Many times it feels like Satan's number one priority for the day is to make me bleed from the wound. Honestly, it's getting harder and harder for him to do. The last thing I would do is to tell you we have experienced phenomenal healing in an unexplainably short amount of time if it wasn't true. I would never put false hope out there. Truth is God has done a work in us that has been completely, 100 percent supernatural. The work he did was and is on his timetable, not defined by man.

Just one and a half years outside of the "bomb" that destroyed everything, I have not had a bad day in nine months. For the past six or seven months, most every time Satan attacks me with thoughts about that night, the emotional response that used to accompany them is dead. I'm talking about pain, resentment, fear, blame, despair, hopelessness, anxiety, depression, heaviness, bitterness, anger, regret, and much more. This "death" is not a perception based on buried feelings and an emotional wall. This "death" was done by the healing hand of God as he covered our emotional wounds. Let me stress this point. The only, and I mean only, part we played in this supernatural healing was a willingness and desperation to be transformed. There was no traditional marriage counseling, marriage conferences, or books. There was just God and obedience when he said, "Take another little step."

The Point

A couple of months before this all came out, God had been speaking to me about where we are supposed to get our validation from. Who is supposed to be the one giving us our sense of self-worth? Who are we supposed to be getting our love from? Who is the one who is supposed to make us feel good about ourselves? Ultimately all of those things are supposed to come from God. God is the one who we need to get our love from. God is the one who tells us who we are. God is the one who makes us feel good about who we are. God provides our sense of self-worth. Basically, everything that we look for our spouse or significant other to provide we are supposed to be getting from God. Does that mean that as a husband, wife, or significant other we do not have to tell our spouses that we love them? Does it mean that we should not show them how much we love and care about them? Absolutely not! However, what it does mean is that we should not allow those compliments and acts of love to become the foundation of what we think about ourselves.

So it had been a couple of weeks since that night and I was replaying a question that I had been asking myself and sort of asking God. That question was: "If we are supposed to be getting everything that we need from God as far as love, self-worth, and validation, then why did he create marriage at all?" If a healthy and healed person gets all of that stuff from God, then why should he/she have to subject himself/herself to marriage where there is pain and suffering? What is the point?

God created marriage as a covenant, right? Why? I was not getting it. In fact, I was getting upset at God. I believe that God designed marriage. I believe that God is in marriage. Or I did believe that anyway. Now I was beginning to question that belief. Can't I experience what you have for me outside of a marriage relationship? That way I am not at risk to experience unimaginable pain and suffering. I would still be at risk of pain and suffering but not the kind that comes when your spouse betrays you. That is the way I thought anyway.

Well, one night I began to ask God that question and not myself anymore. I began to yell at God a little. It was at that point that he interrupted my spewing, as he often does, and gave me the answer. God said to me, "So that you can see me and know me in it." I was very quiet after that as God began to speak more about that to me. The ultimate goal of what God intended marriage to be was a venue where God could reveal who he is to us. The purpose of marriage is for us to be able to reflect God to our spouse in a much deeper way than we can to anyone else in any other relationship. Sounds a little too simple, right? It is a simple statement with simple words. However, those simple words carry quite an impact.

I am sorry if you were expecting a long, drawn out technical purpose with big words. You might say, "Well, can't we reflect God to each other in any relationship that we have?" The answer is yes. You absolutely can, and I am glad you went there if you did. One of the things that I pray God will do with this book is to breach the boundaries of marriage and speak truth into all of our relationships. So yes. You are right. We can and should be reflecting God to everyone we are in relationship with. However, there is something so much deeper in the marriage covenant relationship. Let's look back to the very first man and woman.

> Therefore shall a man leave his father and his mother, and shall cleave unto his wife: and they shall be one flesh.
>
> Genesis 2:24

This verse comes right after Adam explains that Eve was bone of his bones and flesh of his flesh. Then, in the verse that follows verse 24, it states that they were both naked, the man *and his wife,* and they were not ashamed. A marriage covenant relationship is deeper than any other human relationship on earth. We have the chance to experience a level of intimacy that is unavailable anywhere else.

We also have other important passages in Scripture that tell us just how important the marriage covenant is to God. I will list a few of them.

> He that hath the bride is the bridegroom: but the friend of the bridegroom, which standeth and heareth him, rejoiceth greatly because of the bridegroom's voice: this my joy therefore is fulfilled.
>
> John 3:29

In this passage, John the Baptist has just reiterated that he is not the Christ but that he is the one who was sent before him. John states that the one who has the bride, or the church, is the bridegroom, or Jesus. This is a direct comparison between the marriage covenant that God established for us and the relationship Jesus wants with us. We are referred to as the bride. If there was not a much deeper purpose to marriage, God would not have used it to describe the type of relationship he wants to have with us.

In Matthew 9:15, Jesus refers to himself as the bridegroom when questioned about fasting. Jesus asks John's disciples how the guests of the bridegroom can fast while he is with them. Jesus says they will fast when the bridegroom is taken away. We also have the first record of a miracle performed by Jesus being done at a wedding. In Matthew 25 we have the parable of the ten virgins who were to meet the bridegroom. In this parable the kingdom is referred to as a wedding banquet. Here is another:

> And I John saw the holy city, new Jerusalem, coming down from God out of heaven, prepared as a bride adorned for her husband.
>
> Revelation 21:2

Here the new, holy city of Jerusalem is referred to as the bride and God as the husband. That is a beautiful picture. So we see from these passages that the marriage covenant seems to be very important to God. It seems to me that God is saying through this that there is something different in the marriage covenant that he wants to use in a different, deeper way than he uses the rest of our relationships.

It was very important for God to establish the covenant relationship of marriage right from the beginning in the very first man and woman. It was so important for him to do that because God knows it would be very difficult for us to really know and understand his love, acceptance, grace, forgiveness, mercy, and the rest of his characteristics in a tangible way if there was not going to be anything tangible to show us through. That is so true, right? How often do we need to be able to touch or feel something to be able to understand what it is? How often do we need to know with our senses before we can truly understand?

Now is it possible for us to really know and understand the love of God without a marriage relationship? You might point out that, from what we see in the Bible, the apostle Paul was never married, as far as we know, and he had a close relationship with God and seemed to understand who God is. However, we know that there are levels of revelation, and I cannot help but wonder if Paul had experienced a marriage relationship, in the way that God intended it to be, would God have brought him greater revelation and understanding of who God is?

Our ability to really know and understand who God is was so important to God that he created a covenant relationship that could go deeper than other relationships. A covenant where our hearts could be laid bare. A covenant in which our spirits are so intertwined with another that we feel what the other feels. It is a covenant that we can pour our hearts and souls into. We experience what the other experiences. We hurt when they hurt, and we feel joy when they feel joy. It was this covenant relationship in which God chose to reveal to us on a tangible level exactly who he is. The depth of his love and his mountains of grace and forgiveness. And how does he reveal this? Through us!

God shows my wife who he is through me. I see and feel the love that God has for me when my wife touches me. When she encourages me and lifts me up. When she forgives me and shows me grace. When we make love. That last one may sound a little strange, but there is something so deep about the heart of God in making love with your spouse. When I make love with my wife the way that God intended it to be, I get a glimpse into the overwhelming, passionate love of an almighty God.

Follow me on this for just a moment. God created sex. We know that our bodies can only take so much of God. Too much of God would kill us. It would be impossible for our bodies to survive in an extended state of orgasm because during orgasm our bodies are literally taking all they can take. Is it possible that orgasm allows us to tap into a glimpse of the overwhelming passion and pleasure of being in the presence of God? Did God create sex not just for our pleasure but also as a way in which we can come into the presence of a greater portion of God, for just a couple of seconds, than we can any other way? Is there something supernatural about making love with our spouses? If this is true, we have the ability to join with our spouses and experience God like never before.

So what's the point of marriage? To be able to know and understand who God is in a real and tangible way that we do not have in any other relationships. This should be the main reason why we are getting married. All of those reasons from Part A should supplement this.

At the beginning of this book, I set before you a quote from a very well-known author and speaker about the ultimate goal of marriage. Go back and read it again if you need to. I asked the question, "What happens when the union is broken? Where is the provision for that?" I concluded that there was no provision for broken union in that statement. Now let me ask that same question against the goal that I have set before you. What happens when there is betrayal and the covenant of marriage is broken? What happens when your spouse has continuously hurt you and made you feel alone and broken? What happens when you feel that your spouse does not pay attention to you anymore and you are not sure that they still love you? What happens when your spouse has not, despite all of your yelling and nagging, gotten any better at helping you around the house and with the kids? What happens when you realize your spouse isn't who you thought they were? What happens when any or all of the horrible things that you can imagine going wrong in a marriage go wrong?

You reflect God to your spouse. You reflect love. You reflect forgiveness. You reflect compassion, mercy, and grace. You reflect reconciliation, redemption, and restoration. You reflect hope and trust in God. You reflect blessings. You reflect peace and humility. You reflect strength in the Lord. You reflect every single fruit of God's spirit.

It was only by the grace of God, the strength that he gave me, and the healing that I had walked through over the course of a year that I was able to reflect God to Kara when the bomb dropped. Because God had taken me to the place where I could effectively reflect who he is, I was able to reflect love, compassion, forgiveness, grace, and mercy all on the same night. That was absolutely essential to us jumping on the fast track to complete healing.

A great friend of mine who is a pastor in Pennsylvania said, "It is a good thing God is revealed to the world in our marriages. It is also a very unfortunate thing that God is revealed to the world in our marriages." In the pages that follow, I want us to deal a serious blow to the latter part of that statement. It should be a great thing that God is revealed in our marriages, 100 percent of the time.

If you are like me, when you read someone's belief on a goal we should reach, you would ask, "Okay, how do we get there?"

How do we get to a place where we can reflect God to our spouses and in turn be able to reflect who God is in all of our relationships? I am going to tell you how. This is not going to be your typical *twelve steps to a better marriage* strategy. You are not going to hear this at any marriage seminars that I know of. You are also not going to hear this from any well-known and well-published family or marriage therapists that I know of. You will not even hear this in most churches.

What you are going to hear will most likely challenge your theology and may make you very uncomfortable. I will assume that if you have made it this far you most likely have had an open mind, so I encourage you to keep it open because there is real freedom in what I am going to lay before you.

Why Can't We Get There?

I have heard many people ask the question "How do we get there?" in response to a goal set before them. The problem with asking that question is that it puts so much pressure and responsibility on us. When we fail to meet that goal, we have let ourselves down yet again. This is very important when talking about how to improve a marriage.

If you have been to marriage classes and seminars, you have heard the speakers talk to you about how you can make your marriage better. Then at the end they will lay out a strategy filled with practical steps that will take you to the place they think you should be in your marriage. If you have not been to any marriage classes or seminars, I am sure that most of us have heard from a friend or heard in the media somewhere different steps and things you can do to improve your marriage. Another venue famous for practical steps, tools, and exercises is the traditional family therapist and counselor. So we take the paperwork home with us and put into action the things that we have learned. We help our spouses more, and we do more things together. We play to our spouse's "love language" and try to be more considerate. We try things that are meant to improve our communication skills. We begin to read the Bible together and put more emphasis on God in our marriages. We say things like "we need to put God at the center of our marriage." A phrase that has been tossed around so much with no significant meaning attached, I am not sure it even has one.

A friend of mine has this to say:

> We have been to too many meetings where the root issues just were not handled. It was covered over by (it's exposed) but not dealt with. Here it is, here is the mess, but what are we to do about it and what do you do with it? We've done the marriage classes, good for exposure, good for trying (we got the blue ribbon for coming every week), but you just need more. We have too much information this age and not enough action. After the counseling happens, there is a short period of everyone trying to meet the other's need, but the core issues are still there and uncovered and not healed or dealt with. Without the root issues being completely removed, everything will eventually become what it was or worse because Satan does not want this marriage to work.

A couple of months go by, and we start to realize we are not helping our spouses anymore like we were told we should. The paperwork is long gone. We forgot what our spouse's "love language" is, so we cannot play to it. We are communicating just as we used to before we went to the seminars and therapy appointments. We do not read the Bible together anymore, and we are no longer tossing the "put God in the center" statement back and forth. The extra times that we set aside to spend "quality" time together have turned back into watching sports and drinking beer for the men and for the women that longing to spend quality time together is back. Or the other way around, I don't know. To each his or her own. In fact, everything is back to the way it was before you spent I don't know how much to go get those invaluable tools that were supposed to make your marriage better and perhaps save your marriage. Oh, but do not worry. They just announced that there is another marriage seminar coming to town. Maybe that one will really change the dynamic of your marriage, right? Doing the same thing over and over again with the same result, expecting a different result. That is the definition of insanity, right?

There is something very damaging and dangerous to this cycle. You see, it puts all of the pressure and responsibility on us. If we can only follow the steps, then our marriage will be whole and wonderful. When our marriage fails to change, it is not, in our minds, the steps that let us down but us who let us down. How could it be a problem with the material? The speaker is very well known and respected. They have all these testimonies of people whose lives have changed supposedly. So it must be our fault. We are failing. We are failures.

Bitterness and self-hate can easily come from this cycle. The bitterness will attack with accusations that it's all your spouse's fault. If your spouse would take these things seriously, then your marriage would be different, right? We accuse our spouses of not caring about the marriage and not caring about us, and if we don't accuse openly, we accuse them to ourselves. We have worked on what we needed to work on and have done all we can do. We are fixed, and if we only had comparable effort from our spouses, our marriage would be great. There is incredible pride, judgment, bitterness, and resentment in this line of thinking and accusation. It is possible that it has taken a couple of marriage seminar and counseling failures to get you to this point.

Self-hate will attack first with self-blame. "It is not my spouse's fault; it is my fault. This is just another thing in my life I have failed at. I just can't do anything right, and I know my spouse is not happy being married to me. He/she is just waiting for a good time to leave. He/she is probably already having an affair. If I could only keep up with what I learned at the seminar, then I could be a good husband or wife, and it would make him/her happy enough to stay. I am just tired of letting him/her down. I am worthless, and I do not deserve him or her. I am lucky he/she stuck with me this long. There is just no point for me to go to any more marriage seminars or therapy because I am not going to be able to change anything."

Something important to mention here is that bitterness and self-hate were already there before the marriage letdown and perceived failures. Self-blame comes from a root of self-hatred, and accusation comes from a root of bitterness. Both of these roots were there long before any failed marriage seminars.

So now you know why I do not want to ask you, "How do we get there?" I would rather explain to you why we *cannot* get there. This is where things are going to get hairy for many of you. We cannot get there.

We need to lay a little bit of foundation before we dive into this. We need to talk about what sin is. So what is sin? Take a minute and think about it. Sin is anything that goes against what God has taught us, right? Sin is what separates us from God. Sin is … (personal list of offenses). Those are all correct answers to a question; however, they are not the answers to the question I asked. Those are all correct answers if I asked you, "What does sin do?" I asked you, "What is sin?"

> Knowing this, that our old man is crucified with him, that the body of sin might be destroyed, that henceforth we should not serve sin.
>
> Romans 6:6

Paul is talking about sin having a body here and also speaks of the choice we can make to serve this body. Paul is saying here that sin is a *being*. We can make the choice to serve this being; therefore sin can rule over us. Sin is a spiritual *being*. Or a better way I would put it is that sin consists of lots of different spiritual beings or demons. You cannot have a body without many different parts that make up that body. Paul paints a vivid picture of the battle we can have with sin.

> Let not sin therefore reign in your mortal body, that ye should obey it in the lusts thereof.
>
> Romans 6:12

Again, Paul states here that we are not to let sin reign in our bodies. We are not to obey it. We are not to obey this being, this body of sin.

> Know ye not, that to whom ye yield yourselves servants to obey, his servants ye are to whom ye obey; whether of sin unto death, or of obedience unto righteousness?
>
> Romans 6:16

Here Paul again talks about the choice we can make to become servants of sin, and if we make that choice, we become sin's possession.

> But sin, taking occasion by the commandment, wrought in me all manner of concupiscence. For without the law sin was dead.
>
> Romans 7:8

Here Paul is saying that not only is sin a being that can rule over us, but it also has the power to oppress us.

Why is it important that we recognize sin as a being? Because when we can recognize sin as a being, we can get to the next step, which is recognizing that we, as we are, are powerless against it.

> For I know that in me (that is, in my flesh) dwelleth no good thing: for to will is present with me; but how to perform that which is good I find not.
>
> For the good that I would I do not: but the evil which I would not, that I do.

Now if I do that I would not, it is no more I that do it, but sin that dwelleth in me.

I find then a law, that, when I would do good, evil is present with me.

For I delight in the law of God after the inward man:

But I see another law in my members, warring against the law of my mind, and bringing me into captivity to the law of sin which is in my members.

O wretched man that I am! Who shall deliver me from the body of this death?

I thank God through Jesus Christ our Lord. So then with the mind I myself serve the law of God; but with the flesh the law of sin.

Romans 7:18–25

There is a lot here about who or what our fight is against and how we are powerless against it in and of ourselves. Paul states here that he does not know how to perform the good things he wants to do. Paul talks about the fact that he knows the difference between good and evil and really has a passion to do the right thing, but instead he does evil. Paul states that sin, a living being, dwells in him. Paul assigns a law to this and says the law is that wherever there is good, evil is right there also. Paul states there is a law of sin and that law wars with his mind and brings him into captivity by way of his members or body. Paul says that with his mind he serves God but with his body he serves sin. This is an intense battle Paul is describing. He is clearly not fighting against himself but is fighting an outside force that is trying to destroy him. A separate being that is trying to bring destruction, and he is saying that he is powerless against it.

There are two kingdoms that Jesus talks about. We have the kingdom of light and the kingdom of darkness. Jesus is king of the light, and Satan is king of the darkness. Paul talks about not being able to serve both.

> You cannot drink the cup of the Lord and the cup of demons too; you cannot have a part in both the Lord's table and the table of demons.
>
> 1 Corinthians 10:21 (NIV)

We, as humans, are not a kingdom. There are only two kingdoms, therefore only two sources of your thoughts. It is absolutely essential because when you understand this, you can stop fighting yourself and begin to fight the real enemy.

> You have been set free from sin and have become slaves to righteousness.
>
> Romans 6:18 (NIV)

Paul says all throughout this chapter that we are or were slaves to sin. In this passage, he says that we have been set from sin and have become slaves to righteousness. The important part is that we are slaves either way, and there are only two options. We do not fight against ourselves because we are not the originators of anything. We do not come up with anything. We simply make the choice of who we are going to be slaves to on a daily basis.

> For our struggle is not against flesh and blood, but against the rulers, against the authorities, against the powers of this dark world and against the spiritual forces of evil in the heavenly realms.
>
> Ephesians 6:12 (NIV)

Have we forgotten that we are flesh and blood? Our battle is not against ourselves.

Why is it important for us to understand that our fight is not with ourselves? If we can understand this principle, then we can begin to understand that when we step in front of a mirror and the thoughts come that we are ugly and nobody would want us, the thoughts are not coming from us but coming from a very real and vicious enemy we are instructed to fight. When you look at pornography for what seems the millionth time, you can understand you are in bondage, and it is not you that drives you to look at that but is a very real enemy that is driving you to it. When you feel like scum and condemned afterwards, you can realize that's not coming from you either. Condemnation comes from the enemy and conviction comes from the Holy Spirit. Conviction will never tell you that you are a horrible person. Here is a great explanation of the difference:

> Conviction will tell you that there is something wrong with your actions and condemnation will tell you that there is something wrong with you.
>
> Cindy Ackerman

I can't claim responsibility for that piece of wisdom; it was a friend of mine.

Do you ever snap at someone for no good reason? Do you ever wonder why you did that and why you always seem to be angry? When you begin to ask these questions, you can begin to see and understand that the enemy has gained a foothold or stronghold in you. With that awareness you can begin to fight and win back the ground that was lost. When we understand that our battle is not with ourselves, we can begin to let ourselves off the hook and cut ourselves some slack.

Paul faced the same battles, but Paul didn't blame himself. He blamed the body of sin who was attacking him. This does not absolve us of any responsibility for sinning, but it does let us know the bondage we are in is the result of an outside force taking advantage of the choices we make to sin. We have not been fighting a fair battle. We have not been aware of who the enemy is or how to fight his kingdom.

So what are we working toward here? Awareness! We as a body of believers have done a horrible job of being aware of who we are fighting and how to fight. How do we expect to fight a battle much less win a battle with an enemy we aren't even aware of?

One glaring reason for this unawareness is most of us believe that since we have become saved we are totally cleansed and don't have to worry about demonic strongholds and oppression that can and will entangle us. We believe once we are saved we are automatically cleansed and we live free from the bondage of the enemy. What's more is that we are getting this theology from Paul, who never says anything of the sort. I encourage you to look closely at what Paul says. Romans 8:1 says, "There is no condemnation for those who are in Christ Jesus." For those of you who don't know, there is a second part to this verse that the NIV leaves out. It says, "For those who walk after the spirit and not after the flesh." That means that if you walk after the flesh you may be a believer, but you have opened yourself up to attacks of condemnation from the enemy. I will list Romans 6:4 again:

> Therefore we are buried with him by baptism into death: that like as Christ was raised up from the dead by the glory of the Father, even so we also should walk in newness of life.

Here Paul says that we should walk in newness of life even after we were baptized into death with Christ. It is a choice we make every day.

> Likewise reckon ye also yourselves to be dead indeed unto sin, but alive unto God through Jesus Christ our Lord.
> Romans 6:11

Here Paul does not say that we are dead to sin. We are dead to the eternal consequence of sin but not to sin. Paul tells us to reckon ourselves dead to sin. The Greek word for reckon means to estimate or conclude. Paul does not tell us that we are dead to sin, but he tells us to conclude or believe that way. That is a choice we have to make. If we can choose to believe we are dead to sin, it will be a great step in living free from sin.

Knowing this, that our old man is crucified with him, that the body of sin might be destroyed, that henceforth we should not serve sin.

Romans 6:6

Our old man is crucified that the body of sin *might* be destroyed that we *should* not serve sin. Paul never says that the body of sin is destroyed and never says that we do not serve sin. Paul says we should not serve sin, implying that I can believe in Jesus and become saved at the cross, but I can make a decision to serve sin the next day. In Romans 7 Paul states that there are times when he serves sin. No one is going to argue whether or not Paul was saved at the time of that writing. In fact, Paul saw the light of God and heard his voice on the way to Damascus, and it still didn't matter. Paul uses this language all throughout Romans. Paul never states or implies we are cleansed at the cross.

Let me share with you some things that I have noticed. I became a Christian at a very young age. I have told you some of the struggles that I have faced over the years. All of those addictions and struggles latched on to me *after* I was saved. If I was cleansed at the cross, then I should have never had to deal with any addictions, right? Why are alcoholics still alcoholics after they get saved? Why do porn addicts still look at pornography after they are saved? Why do drug addicts still use drugs after they are saved? Why do bitter people still hold bitterness after they are saved? Why do people that do not love themselves still hate themselves after they are saved? Why do people who are ruled by fear still have stress, worry, anxiety, and dread after they are saved? Because we are not cleansed at the cross; we have only begun at that point.

Now there are some of you ... okay, okay, let's be real. There are a whole lot of you that will fight me to the bitter end on my theology of not being cleansed at the cross. I am not going to tell all of you who disagree that you are wrong. I cannot tell you that simply because we do not see a definite answer in Scripture either way on this matter. The best any of us has in this argument are opinions that come from our interpretations, and so it would be arrogant of me to tell you that you are completely wrong in your opinion. On the flip side, I believe that it would be equally wrong for you to tell me that I am completely wrong in mine.

I do have one question for all of you who disagree with me on this matter. This question is specifically aimed at those of you who constantly struggle with pornography, drugs/alcohol, masturbation, rage, inability to be emotionally intimate, gambling, depression, bitterness, inability to be who you want to be, eating disorders, overeating, and whatever else you're consumed by. The question is how is your theology helping you with these issues? Is your theology telling you that you got cleansed from all of these things at the cross? It is telling you that all strongholds were washed away when you came to accept Christ as your Lord and Savior. Then why does it seem like we cannot overcome these issues in our lives? Is it because our relationship with God needs to grow more? We need to know him more and make him more involved in our lives, right? How do we do that? Well, we pray more and have more quiet time and sometimes fast and don't forget to read the Bible every day. Let me ask you ... how is that going for you? Is it working? Are you free? Be honest! Have you experienced a short season of rest from temptation only to have it come crashing back stronger than ever?

The most common scheme that I have seen come from this is bitterness toward God and also intense feelings of rejection by God. What else can the result be? You pray, fast, read the Word, have lots of quiet time, go to church, and the constant struggles remain. You wail at God and plead with him to take it away from you, and still you struggle. The conclusion becomes that God is not listening and does not care and/or there is something wrong with you because God is rejecting you. Condemnation comes onto you and tells you that you are not spending enough time with God or fasting enough or reading the Bible enough.

Beloved, I have been on your side of this theological issue, and I know how all of these things feel. It makes us feel like crap. It is hard work trying to do enough spiritually so that God will take away our struggles. Aren't you tired of feeling this way? I know I was. Aren't you tired of feeling rundown and beat up? Aren't you tired of feeling like you are just barely holding on in the fight against your constant struggle? Aren't you tired of falling again and again and again and feeling like you don't have control? Does it have to get to a point of complete and utter desperation before you are willing to consider another way you may be healed? Do you have to continue to pelt the people you love with the consequences of your constant struggles for years and years before you are willing to consider a different way? Are you willing to put your theology on the shelf and try something new?

You may say, "Jesse, why don't you put your theology on the shelf and try our side of this issue?" That is fair. I have already lived on your side of this theological issue and remained in bondage and allowed new bondage in. Now I invite you to step onto the side of this issue that I have found freedom in through Christ Jesus my Lord and Savior.

We carry the strongholds we had before we got saved right into life after we got saved, and most of us pick up a couple extra along the way. I certainly picked up a lot. Salvation is a gift that is our responsibility to appropriate. We have all the tools; we just are not aware of them. Can a Christian have a demon? Not only can we have demons, but we were born with them and have been living with them our whole life. They have been comfortable in us because we do not recognize and choose not to believe they are there. That makes it impossible to live free from things like fear, bitterness, unforgiveness, and self-hate. These are, by the way, some of the main blocks that are keeping you from getting to the place in your marriage and other relationships that God intended for you to be.

Why is awareness so important to the battle? Because when we become aware of whom the battle is against we can separate ourselves from sin and separate others from sin, and that is the first step in gaining freedom.

This should be very encouraging for us. No longer do we have to think that there is something wrong with us. No longer do we have to wonder if we are just not strong enough to overcome our struggles. That if we could only pray more and maybe fast then God would deliver us from our struggles. Relax and take a deep breath. It is your responsibility that you made and continue to make the choice to sin. However, it is not your fault that you are constantly pushed that way, and it is not your fault that you have not been able to overcome the sin. It is not your fault that you have so much trouble opening to your spouse. It is not your fault that you constantly feel anger toward your spouse or sometimes have flashes of rage against them. It is not your fault that you constantly worry. It is not your fault that even though you try hard, you just cannot get to the place you want to be in your marriage. The problems that you see on the surface have deep roots. You have just not been aware. Now you are, and now we can expose and eliminate the enemy that has been allowed to operate in your life.

So why can't we get there? The reason is that we are in bondage and the enemy has a stranglehold on us. We have been that way from birth.

> Behold, I was shapen in iniquity; and in sin did my mother conceive me.
>
> Psalm 51:5

This is David stating the fact that we are born into bondage. We are born into sin. We are born at a disadvantage. The problem is that we do not even know it. Let's change that.

Our hope for restored marriages rests in our willingness and ability to be individually transformed. Our relationships will not be transformed until we are transformed individually. Transformation can only happen when we move beyond our desperation that says "I can't live one more day without relief from my current circumstance" into the desperation that says "I cannot survive one more day without the overwhelming love and presence of God saturating my entire being." Many are desperate for the former; few are desperate for the latter. The type of desperation we need is only ignited by God when we are ready to lay down everything, and I mean everything, in our lives. That includes being willing to question every piece of theology and belief system we have learned along the way. Are you that desperate?

The Unloving

Before we go any further, I would like to say something. Demons. Demons. Demons. Demons. Demons. Okay, now that we have that out of the way, we can move on. I want you to be comfortable with that word because I am going to be using it in the pages ahead. We are going to be talking about three groups of them over the next three chapters. I feel that these three are important because they are responsible for denying us the ability to reflect God to our spouses. The three that we are going to deal with are the spirits, or demons, of the unloving, bitterness, and fear.

It is important that we deal with the unloving first because it is a very big block in our marriages. The unloving was the main block and reason why I could not totally open up to my wife and why she could not totally open up to me. The unloving is also the main reason why the enemy, or Satan, was able to work a scheme of unfaithfulness in my wife. What we call the "unloving" is nothing more than a group of demons with specific functions.

What Is It?

The demons of the "unloving" are as follows:

- Self-unforgiveness
- Self-bitterness
- Rejection and self-rejection
- Self-resentment
- Self-anger
- Self-violence
- Self-wrath
- Self-hatred
- Self-murder

I heard an analogy that I am going to repeat now. It described how Satan attacks us. Picture an ant crawling across a table in a restaurant. We would get rid of the ant with a napkin or our thumbs, right? Satan would blow up the entire restaurant just to kill that ant. With that in mind, I bring to your awareness three more spirits that come to join the party. They are:

- Shame
- Guilt
- Condemnation

It would be nice if that were all of them, right? Hold on. Remember the ant? There is one more that comes in.

- Accusation

So this is *what* the demons of the unloving are.

What Does It Do?

This is a very important question. Many of you are scratching your heads right now wondering if there is any truth to what I am saying. You may be saying that I am "out there." I can tell you that I believe that all of my knowledge in this area has been revelation from God, and I believe he has used three different avenues to teach me. The three are the Bible, other people, and personal experience. My prayer is that as I share with you what these demons do, some connections will be made between some things that you have struggled with your whole life and finally a reason why they have not gone away despite your best efforts.

- Self-unforgiveness
- Self-bitterness
- Rejection and self-rejection
- Self-resentment
- Self-anger
- Self-violence
- Self-wrath
- Self-hatred
- Self-murder

These demons are the foundation to why we hate ourselves. The spirit of rejection plays one of the biggest roles here. Rejection is a lie. Every single time rejection is a lie. The pain is real, but no one has the power to reject you as a person. For example, I am sure that most of us have experienced the hurt that comes with a boy or girl that we have feelings for not having the same feelings back. I experienced that pain more than once in my younger days. The times we are hurting from other people choosing not to reflect back the feelings we wish they would is a great time for rejection to come and lie to us. Rejection will tell us not only that we have been rejected but that we *are* rejected. See, the people who hurt us were not rejecting us as people; they were just rejecting us as their significant other. But we don't see it that way. We listen to the lie that they have rejected us as people so therefore we are rejected. As a result, we are easy targets for the lies to come about how ugly and undesirable we are. We listen and believe the lies that if we only worked out more or if only we were smarter we could have been with that person who hurt us. See how quickly a perceived rejection of us as people spiraled right down into self-rejection.

This scheme plays out so many times in a person's life, and as we become more and more entangled in this scheme, the truth that we are accepted as people by God is not enough for us. We have to find our validation in people because they are who have hurt us. As we continue to try to be validated by people, we continue to fall victim to the scheme of rejection time after time. As we begin to live in self-rejection, that bondage wears us down deeper and deeper until we are passed off to the demon of self-hatred.

This is not the only scheme of rejection; this was just a very obvious one. There are plenty more. Most of us walk around every day either feeling rejected or living in fear of rejection. The main function of the spirit of rejection is to get you to believe the lie that you *are* rejected. Once we are there, we are easy targets for the rest.

There are other ways that we can get to self-rejection and self-hatred. We, as humans, have a tendency to be very hard on ourselves. Did you ever stop and wonder why that is? Could it be possible that we really want to forgive ourselves but when we try and go there we are so bombarded by the lies of *shame, guilt,* and *condemnation* that we just cannot? I have done many things over the course of my life that I am not proud of. I have sinned in many different ways. I have done things that have really hurt other people as well as myself. It was not easy to forgive myself for some of those things. Why is that? Why is it that when we do something that really disappoints someone we care about or causes tremendous pain to ourselves and/or others it is so hard to forgive ourselves? Enter in self-bitterness and self-unforgiveness.

When we do things we are really not happy with ourselves for, we get very angry at ourselves. Have you ever said, "I can't believe that I did that"? How about when we tell ourselves that we are so stupid for doing that thing we hate doing again? How about when a person gets drunk and sleeps with someone he or she had no intention of sleeping with? How about when you have another one-night stand after telling yourself you were not going to be that person anymore? How about living with the pain of having had an abortion? What about the people who have said they would never do drugs, gamble, or look at pornography again? How about when we cheat on our spouses or just cheat on any relationship?

What if I told you that when we say, "I am so stupid," "All I do is disappoint people who care about me," "I am not strong enough to overcome this," "I am tired of letting people down," "I do not deserve to be forgiven because of what I have done," that those words started as thoughts and you are not the one that put them in your mind? What if I told you that the demon of self-bitterness plants those lies in our minds and just waits for us to accept them? We fall victim to this scheme time after time. We believe these lies and fall into bondage of self-bitterness, and as an added bonus for the enemy, we are at that point under bondage to the demon of self-unforgiveness, and as long as we continue not to forgive ourselves, we cannot live in the love God wants to show us. Self-bitterness will quickly pass us off to self-rejection and then to self-hatred. To go along with self-bitterness, we also begin to resent ourselves for the pain that we cause. Now self-resentment has a hold on us.

Self-anger and self-violence are things that we can go to on the way to self-hatred, and as I said before, the ultimate goal of these demons is to get you to self-murder. What self-murder will do to you is obvious. News.softpedia.com reports that there are over one million suicides in the world every year. This site reports that number is higher than the number of people killed in wars, terrorist attacks, and homicides. Are we ready to admit there is a powerful scheme at work here? Are we finally ready to become aware and start winning some battles? I hope so because that statistic is very disturbing.

- Shame
- Guilt
- Condemnation

These three demons I view as the keepers of the foundation of the unloving. These demons wait around in silence until they feel threatened. When they can sense that there is a danger of one the foundation pieces falling, they will spring into action. These three have the ability to knock us down very quickly. There may have been many times over the course of your life that you would have had victory over the unloving if it were not for these three.

These demons use the things you have done over the course of your life to bring such an onslaught of shame, guilt, and condemnation that you can hardly breathe. These demons will also attack through anyone who tells you "you should be ashamed of yourself." These three get most of their power to be effective from accusation. I don't know if there is much more to say about what these three do. We all know what shame, guilt, and condemnation feel like. We can all agree they're not our favorite set of feelings.

- Accusation

I view accusation as the demon who acts as a keeper for shame, guilt, and condemnation and as one that supplies power to those three. Accusation, like rejection, is made up entirely of lies. Satan is called "the accuser of the brethren," and we are constantly being accused.

Accusation is the demon who is feeding your mind with the lies that you are ugly, worthless, not worthy of love, undesirable, a failure, unlovable, a bad mother, a bad father, or a bad son/daughter. Accusation tells you that you have been rejected by God and that God does not care about you. Accusation tells you that you are not good enough and that you don't measure up. Accusation will act as an instant-replay service and replay, in your mind, the things you are most ashamed of, whether they be things you did or things that happened to you. Accusation will then take those things and tell you that you are a horrible person and that you do not deserve forgiveness. Or accusation will tell you that you deserved what happened to you and that it's your fault. Accusation will tell you that you will never find anyone to love you. It will tell you that your spouse does not love you and that you are not even worthy of being loved. It tells you that if you do not keep your spouse happy then he/she will leave you.

When you fall back into a repetitive sin, accusation will tell you that you are scum and that you will never overcome the problem. It will tell you that your spouse would be better off without you and that there is someone better than you out there for him or her. It will tell you everyone would be better off if you were dead.

Every single negative thing that comes into your mind telling you how horrible you are comes from accusation. When we believe these lies we slip further and further into bondage. These thoughts are not coming from you; they are coming from an outside source, and it is time to stand up and face that source.

The only power these demons of the unloving have exists in our being unaware of who our fight is against and how to fight that battle. I have not met one person yet in ministry who was not in bondage to the unloving demons. In fact, I will be bold enough to say that most of us live in some degree of bondage to the unloving. Praise God it only takes the mention of the name of Jesus and that bondage is shattered. Here are some characteristics I have seen in people who are in bondage to the unloving:

- Are driven
- Do not want to be touched
- Have a hard time receiving nonsexual intimate touch

- Have a hard time sharing feelings and being vulnerable
- Do not receive compliments
- Live in fear, stress, worry, and dread
- Have a hard time showing love
- Get very irritated when people ask personal questions
- Find validation in people or work
- Let people take advantage of them so they will be liked
- Fear failure and letting people down
- Have addictions of any kind

When we are in bondage to the unloving spirits, we are also giving the enemy rights to cause problems in our bodies. Most autoimmune diseases can be rooted in self-hatred. We have also found that many types of arthritis seem to be rooted in self-hatred. There are many others as well.

I will talk very briefly and I do mean very briefly about the foundation of what I have just said. It has been medically proven that there are chemicals and hormones that are released when the hypothalamus is stimulated by what Pastor Henry Wright calls "stinkin' thinkin'." When we think negatively about ourselves, the hypothalamus is stimulated and releases the chemicals and hormones that are responsible for many diseases and conditions. I wish I could tell you more. We have seen God heal autoimmune disease and arthritis and other diseases as the unloving spirits were dealt with. As people were healed spiritually, God healed them physically. Glory to God!

Where Does It Come from?

You shall not bow down to them or worship them; for I, the LORD your God, am a jealous God, punishing the children for the sin of the fathers to the third and fourth generation of those who hate me.

Exodus 20:5 (NIV)

Is it possible that it is not entirely our fault that we are in the bondage to the unloving that we are in? Is it possible that because the people in our generational line were in bondage to the unloving that we started out in bondage to the same thing? According to this passage, the answer is yes. This verse is also repeated in Deuteronomy 5:9 and Exodus 34:7. God is saying that he will punish the children for the iniquity of the fathers to the third and fourth generation. You might say if that is true than the third and fourth generations are long gone so you should not be affected. Consider this. If there has been sexual sin in your family line, for example, one of your distant relatives had committed rape, it is very possible that there is a curse of sexual immorality on your generational line. Let's say all of your ancestors stayed clear of all types of sexual immorality for two generations but that third generation committed some type of sexually immoral sin. Now the curse is extended from that point another three or four generations and so on. From that perspective, it is easy to see how curses could have made it all the way into your life.

It is the same thing with the curse of the unloving. If your parents did not like themselves very much, you can take it to the bank that you were born into the unloving curse. My parents were born into this bondage, and I was born into this bondage.

Now, you may also be saying, "God punishes for sin. How does not loving yourself fit into that?" That is a fair question. In my experience in ministry, there have been very few people who recognize not loving yourself as a sin. Is it? Let us take a look at what Jesus says about this question.

> "'Honor your father and mother,' and 'love your neighbor as yourself.'"
>
> Matthew 19:19 (NIV)

I heard a speaker once say that if we find something in the gospels that is repeated in the other gospels, then it is very important and we should pay close attention. This verse is repeated in Mark 12:31 and Luke 10:27. So we should pay close attention, right? Hold on. It is also repeated in Romans 13:9, Galatians 5:14; and in James 2:8, it is referred to as "The royal law." This is not a suggestion; it is a command. We are commanded to honor our parents *and* love our neighbors as we love ourselves. We are commanded to love ourselves. When we are walking in self-hate, we are turning our backs on a commandment from God, and therefore we are walking in sin.

We have no right to hate ourselves because God loves us. How can we walk in blessings and fulfilling relationships when we hate what God loves? I will not drum this down at all. When we walk in self-hatred, we are choosing to walk in disobedience and rebellion to God, and we can expect consequences for our sin. We have established that the root of the unloving is sin, so we can establish it can be passed down through the generations and into our lives.

Where else can bondage to the unloving come from? We give rights to the unloving to hold us in bondage with the sin we willingly enter into over the course of our lives. For example, a young woman has been brought up in the church and has been told that sex before marriage is fornication and that fornication is sin. So the young woman goes out and meets a boy. They start to date, and one night things go too far and they end up having sex. The young woman is torn inside with guilt, shame, and condemnation because she did something that she had been taught not to do her whole life and she cannot take it back. She holds herself in unforgiveness and self-hate.

This is true for most sins that we commit. So many times we are so unwilling to let ourselves off of the hook. It does not matter if we steal, lie, cheat, fight, murder, look at pornography, or engage in sexual immorality in any other way. We hold on to our guilt and shame, and we invite the demons of the unloving to come in and strangle us. We allow them to suck out our joy and energy.

There is one other avenue through which the unloving demons can gain access to us. This avenue is through the acts of others. I know those of you that have been sexually abused would say there is no way people can feel that level of shame, guilt, and condemnation unless they themselves have been sexually abused. I am going to tell you that the demons of the unloving attack each person the same way. A person who has been told by their parents or people at school that they are ugly and worthless feels the intensity of shame and guilt just the same as someone who has been sexually abused. My point is there is not just one avenue available to the enemy to bring a devastating attack of all the unloving properties. There are a handful of avenues, and each one feels devastating to the target.

How Does It Affect My Marriage?

You may be saying, "This is all well and good, but what does it have to do with my marriage?" I am glad you asked because I want to tell you. Bondage to the unloving is the most destructive bondage to our marriages. Here is the reason why. When we are in bondage to the unloving, we are unable to really know and understand the perfect love of God. There may have been and probably have been times in your life that you have experienced the love of God. You may have been at some kind of conference or at church or even by yourself and God just poured his love down on you. It may have been an amazing time for you. What happened the next day? Did you still feel that love? What about a couple of days later? Did you even remember what that experience felt like, or did you forget most of it?

What happens is that there are times in our lives when God shows us his love and we feel like we really know God, but by the time the next day rolls around, the unloving has stolen that moment and we go back to life as normal. We forget the feeling, and we forget the perfect love of God. That perfect love never makes it to our spirits to stay, so we walk through life with an experience here and there but never with the constant knowledge and understanding of God's perfect love for us. Thus we miss out on life the way that God truly wants us to live it. To live without understanding the constant perfect love of God is a devastating way to live. I lived in this way for twenty-six years. We will never be able to have the type of relationship that we want with God, let alone our spouses, until we deal with the unloving bondage that we are in. Here is why:

> We love him, because he first loved us.
>
> 1 John 4:19

We only have the ability to love because God first loved us. Love comes from God. If we cannot understand the perfect love of God, how can we truly love at all? The answer is that we cannot. How can we exist in a marriage in which neither of the partners really understands love? Well, looking at the marriage statistics, I would say we really are not living in our marriages.

The unloving bondage will not allow us to understand love, and therefore it will not allow us to really understand how to love our spouses. As a result, we will not open up with our spouses to the point of being totally laid bare before them. When we are in bondage to this spirit, it is impossible to really open up to our spouses because first of all we do not really understand how our spouses could love us and second because if we are totally open with them and show vulnerability in every area of our lives, then any reason our spouses married us would be gone and that would be it. They would leave. We try to protect the reasons we feel our spouses could love us and chose to marry us. Much of the time, that "protection" makes us emotionally unavailable, and it does not allow our spouse to see who we really are. The unloving does not even give us a chance to let our spouses love the real us because it uses so much fear of rejection to prevent it.

It is not that we are choosing not to love our spouses; it is just that we cannot because we do not know love ourselves. This lack of understanding will spill over into every dimension of our marriage relationships. One of the most destructive areas it spills into is sexual intimacy. If we really have no understanding of love, what in the world makes us think that when we are sexually intimate with our spouses we are making love with them?

What does it mean to make love? Does it mean getting out the candles and going slower? Does it mean rose petals, champagne, and satin sheets? That is what I used to think. Oh, you want to make love this time? Okay, let's change some environmental things and alter the routine a little, and *Presto!* We are making love. I hope that sounds as ridiculous as I intended to make it sound. Does changing superficial things give us an understanding of what love is? How can we make something that we do not understand? We would all agree that "making love" should feel different that just having sex. Can you tell the difference between the two in your spirit and soul? After you get past the changes that were made, does "making love" feel like "having sex" with a different look, smell, and sound?

I don't believe God ever intended sexual intimacy to be anything but "making love." However, most of us don't know how to truly "make love" because we don't really understand love. I am not saying that there is anything evil or wrong about candles, sheets, and music. My point is that if you are expecting those things to take your sexual intimacy to the next level, you and your spouse are going to be very disappointed and unfulfilled.

The unloving works in both partners and destroys any chance of real unity and intimacy. Over the first four years of my marriage, I had a nagging concern that I really did not know who I was married to. I know Kara felt the same way. Off the top of my head, I cannot remember any time during the first four or five years that I got a glimpse of who Kara really was. I never felt like I got more than a glimpse of real emotion that went deeper than just tears or laughter. I was not allowed inside to stay. It was the same way for her as she lived with me. Communication was, for the most part, superficial. There was not much talk about real emotion. I don't believe that we had a bad relationship; there was just not much depth. We were doing the best that we knew how to do in our brokenness and our woundedness.

So how does the unloving affect our marriages? It destroys our ability to understand love, which, in turn, destroys our ability to love. That destroys our ability to be totally open and laid bare before our spouses, and that will destroy deep and intimate communication. It will also destroy our ability to "make love" with our spouses. As your marriage goes on over the years, there will be a void or barrier between the two of you that you do not understand. You may feel lonely. You may feel that your spouse does not open up to you. That will make you feel that you do not even truly know him/her.

I will share my own testimony of walking free from the unloving bondage. I had lived my whole life listening to people talk about God's love and reading about it in the Bible. However, I did not feel like it was real for me. I had experienced God's love at times, but it never stuck with me. There was an experience that I had at a Promise Keepers event, and I really felt the love of God on me. It was great. The next day I did not feel that love anymore, and I was back to living the way I had been living all along and that was wondering if God really does love me. I remember I would ask myself and wonder why I could not feel the way I felt at the conference all of the time. Why did I not always feel the love of God? There were times at church on Sunday morning I really felt God's love, but by the time Monday rolled around or even Sunday afternoon, I had forgotten that feeling. There was some comfort in what I had heard leaders say many times in "be careful not to live for the spiritual highs because they do not stay." There was comfort in that because it showed me what I was experiencing was a normal thing, but I was beginning to get hungry for more.

God shifted the course of my life one morning, and a couple of months later I was walking through healing for the unloving bondage. I know that was a rapid jump, but all of the things that I walked through over those months would fill another book. Suffice it to say that God did a lot and opened my eyes. The day after I had dealt with the unloving bondage at Operation Light Force, I was spending some time alone with God, and I was asking for new revelations of his love for me. Suddenly I was overcome with God's love in a way that I had never experienced. It drove me to my knees and then onto my face. I could feel the weight of it on me. It saturated my entire being. I was filled with such emotion that I started to cry. It was incredible. The joy and peace was amazing. I said, "God, I want more! Give me more! I want it all!"

God spoke and said, "Jesse, if I were to pour out all of my love on you, it would kill you." God is love. God was pouring out himself onto me. When Paul talks about the love of God that surpasses all knowledge, he is not just making a cute little analogy, but he is saying that we really cannot understand or comprehend the full love of God. To know love is to know God. We as humans can get a glimpse, but we cannot comprehend it all.

That was an amazing experience, and from that point on things began to change in me. Suddenly the scripture I had read about who I am in Christ and what God thinks about me came to life. It started to speak to my spirit. I began to change the way I was with Kara. I was open. I was unafraid to be vulnerable in every area. I was done protecting myself. I started to talk about feelings and started to truly love my wife. I was finally beginning to have the relationship with God I had always wanted and the type of marriage that I always wanted. I found I actually wanted to spend lots of time with Kara. I just wanted to be with her. I found that I wanted to share my day with her, and when she would ask me questions, I wanted to answer them and didn't feel like she was intruding.

A couple of months after my experience with God's love, I was spending some time with God by myself, and I had a vision. I saw a man on a beach. Every so often a large wave would come and crash over the man, and then the water would recede. However, even though the water receded, the sand was still wet that the man was standing on. The Lord spoke and said, "This is what my love is like free from bondage. There are specific times when I pour out my love onto my people in power and it leaves them totally drenched (the waves). That feeling does not last forever and it recedes. However, their spirits (sand) are still wet with the knowledge of my love and it never dries out." When we walk in God's love, free from bondage, we walk with the constant knowledge and understanding of his love for us. That does not mean that we will always feel the power of it, but what it does mean is that we will never forget it.

After I had been hurt in my marriage the way that I had been, I had to do serious battle with the unloving for the first time. I had gone through ministry months before that, but it was the first time I really had to decide if I was going to fight or just fall back into the bondage I had been in. I would have much rather had an easier first test, but it is what it is. I had to do some serious battle with rejection, self-blame, self-resentment, validation, and accusation. Thank God that he had given me the tools I needed to fight those battles because without God I would not have made it through that winter. Every time I got attacked with one of those weapons, it almost took me out. It took my breath away. I give glory to God for sticking with me.

I encountered a Christian woman one time in ministry who had been walking in self-hatred for sixty years. This person was dealing with a handful of medical problems, and she had come to us at Operation Light Force for help. Through the leading of the Holy Spirit, we discerned that the unloving was in operation and began to minister into it. As God led us through the roots of the bondage, I took authority over the spirit of accusation. When I told that spirit to leave, this woman's face changed and her voice became much lower, and the demon started to manifest through this woman through moaning and shaking. Over the next couple of weeks, God used us to deal with every spirit of the unloving, and today this woman is walking in freedom. She is laughing and smiling. She said that prior to ministry she could not remember the last time that she was really happy. She now loves herself and is enjoying the relationship with God that she always wanted. Praise God!

There are many other testimonies that I have had the privilege of bearing witness to. Kara walked through healing from the unloving, and today we enjoy a relationship that I never thought was possible between two people.

* * *

From Kara:

So, as you all know, Jesse and I got married very young. I was only nineteen. I was in shape and excited to simply enjoy the new freedoms of being married. This all changed on an October day, only two months after getting married. God surprised us with the fact that I was eight weeks pregnant. My body changed rapidly, and I no longer fit into my clothes. My self-image took a turn for the worst, not that I ever had high self-esteem.

I can't remember ever truly feeling like I loved myself. I saw this as a form of pride and went in the complete opposite direction of that. If I got honest, I would have to say I hated myself. I could not look into the mirror without first picking out the things that I found repulsive. The unloving deepened in me through every cutting remark, bodily change, and rejection by various people. I sought out validation in any place that I could find it, specifically in the opposite sex. I longed to fill the void that I felt. I was not aware that this void could only be filled by accepting God's love for me and by, in turn, loving myself. I ran straight into the arms of unhealthy friendships and bad boyfriends. Did this help the problem? Not a chance—with every wrong decision, I only fell deeper into the unloving.

For me, the unloving spirits that held me in bondage were

self-unforgiveness, self-bitterness, self-rejection, self-resentment, and self-hatred. After the affair, take those five, multiply
them by a million, and also add self-anger, self-violence, and
yes, even self-murder. The ways that these spirits manifested
were that I had a hard time sharing feelings and being vulnerable; did not receive compliments; lived in fear, stress, worry,
and dread; had a hard time showing love; let people take advantage of them so that I would be liked; and had fear of failure and
letting people down.

Everyone has different ways of being exposed to and opening doors to the unloving. In my life, I feel there were some
things passed down generationally, an incomplete knowledge of
the perfect love of God, the idea that love is earned, and most
significantly, rejection.

On a side note, I feel that is important to share that in no
way when I express some of my opinions or testimonies am I
attempting to justify or place blame on anyone or thing but
myself for my actions. I am very aware that even when we are
exposed to these things, we are always given a way out. As the
Bible says, "There hath no temptation taken you but such as is
common to man: but God is faithful, who will not suffer you
to be tempted above that ye are able; but will with the temptation also make a way to escape, that ye may be able to bear it"
(1 Corinthians 10:13).

After dealing with the unloving spirits in my life, I am able
to look into the mirror and see someone who is beautiful, holy,
pure, a daughter of the King, a princess. All of my relationships,
at least from my perspective of them, have drastically changed
for the better. My relationship with Jesse is an absolutely incredible thing. I am able to receive and give love like I never thought
possible. The love that I feel from and for Jesse now literally
makes my heart swell. I am overwhelmed by the intimacy that
we are now able to share. I am, for the first time, able to separate
true intimacy from physical intimacy. I look at Jesse and can
see glimpses of who God is through him. He is my helper, he is

my best friend (besides God, of course), he is my lover, and he is a wonderful father to my children. Most importantly, I now have the ability to be in a true relationship with the God of the universe. I love my Daddy; he is so wonderful and merciful and is refining daily. It is only by his grace that I am able to be on this journey with my marriage still intact. Thank you, Father!

. . .

The unloving is an epidemic today. I cannot think of a single person that has come in for ministry who has not needed ministry for the unloving. It is destroying our marriages and our relationships. It is also keeping us from enjoying relationship with God. Enough is enough! Let's deal with this and get on with everything that God has for us.

Fear

Fear is the second of the three that we are going to discuss. It's important to deal with after the unloving because without knowing the perfect love of God in your spirit, it is impossible to walk free from fear.

> There is no fear in love; but perfect love casteth out fear: because fear hath torment. He that feareth is not made perfect in love.
>
> 1 John 4:18

If we do not know perfect love, how can we expect to walk free from fear?

What Is It?

> For God hath not given us the spirit of fear; but of power, and of love, and of a sound mind.
>
> 2 Timothy 1:7

I know that most of us have heard this verse many times. Unfortunately, very few people really understand it. Have you ever taken the time to closely examine this passage? If you did, you will discover that fear is a spirit. The Greek word used here for spirit is *pneuma,* meaning angel, daemon (or demon), and God. This passage states that God did not give us the spirit of fear, so that takes care of the word spirit meaning God or any angels from God. That leaves daemon or demon. So first, fear is a demon or evil spirit.

Secondly, fear is a sin. Does that surprise you? I have noticed that there are few people who recognize fear as a sin. In the Bible, we are commanded 144 times to "fear not." We are commanded, "Be not afraid," fifty-four times. When we violate a command from God, we are walking in rebellion and in disobedience to him. We can all agree on that. Fear is the opposite of faith. There is a holy and reverent fear that we are to have of God, but that is not what we are talking about here.

So then the question is what differentiates the godly fear from the ungodly fear? Ungodly fear is made up of four parts.

- Stress
- Anxiety
- Worry
- Dread

Have you ever recognized stress, anxiety, worry, and dread as being the same as fear? These four things are interchangeable with fear. If you break down any situation in which you have experienced any one of those four, you will find yourself in fear very quickly. God even addresses anxiety, worry, and dread specifically.

Then I said unto you, Dread not, neither be afraid of them.
Deuteronomy 1:29

Do not be anxious about anything, but in everything, by prayer and petition, with thanksgiving, present your requests to God.

Philippians 4:6

Therefore do not worry about tomorrow, for tomorrow will worry about itself. Each day has enough trouble of its own.

Matthew 6:34

So anxiety, worry, stress, and dread are all fear. I encourage you to consider this. I have said before that awareness is the first step to defeating an enemy, so I hope that we all can become aware of what fear really is so that we can defeat it.

Where Does It Come from?

Fear gets a stronghold in us from a couple of different avenues. The first one is generational bondage. As I reflected on my family tree, I began to realize that fear had run rampant through my generations. Growing up, my house was ruled by fear. My father and mother lived in fear, and it was passed down to my sisters and me.

Fear gains a right in our lives as a result of our actions. Not only do many of us start out with strongholds of fear from our ancestors, we reinforce it with the choices we make over the course of our lives. Every time we watch horror movies we allow fear into our lives. Every time we worry about the finances we allow fear into our lives. When we worry about where our kids are and what they might be doing, we allow fear into our lives. There is wisdom in knowing where our kids are, who they are with, and setting boundaries. There is sin in constantly worrying about them instead of entrusting them to God. Every time we try to present our families and homes to others as "perfect" because we fear rejection, we allow fear into our lives. Every time we pull back from letting our spouses see who we really are, we allow fear into our lives. Every single thing we have participated in linked to the occult, no matter how small, has given fear a wide open door into our lives.

Fear comes from traumatic events. Traumatic accidents often open a door to a spirit of fear, and we are left with the fear that the same thing is going to happen again and that we will never heal. We are left with the fear that the next time we have an accident it will kill us.

There are different avenues fear takes to enslave us, but the biggest open door for fear is the inability to understand the perfect love of God in our spirits. Perfect love casts out fear. If we don't know love, we don't have a chance against fear. To walk free from fear means total trust in God. If we don't understand God's love for us, we are not going to be able to trust him. Without faith it is impossible to please God. Faith is born from perfect love. The truth is if there is any fear in your life, no matter what it is, there is a lack of understanding and revelation of the perfect love of God. Since God is love, if we are living in fear we don't really know God.

What Does Fear Do?

I will sum up what fear does in one word—*control*. Fear makes its living trying to control anything and everything around it. Fear loves to be in charge because then it can try to control the atmosphere of everything. Fear will rule you with stress, anxiety, worry, and dread, driving you to do whatever you can to prevent bad things from happening. What are some things fear leads us to try to control? Fear will lead us to try to control our spouses, kids, jobs, homes, and even God.

When fear is a part of our lives, we will try to control our spouses. We will begin to tell them what to wear, where to go, and what to do. They will spend money the way we tell them to. They will do what we want and when we want them to do it. We say when they can go out with their friends and what time to be home. They will be the ones to watch the kids so that we can do whatever we want whenever we want. We will also be the ones who determine how often we make love and when we want it we get it. We are the ones who always get what we want.

Now these things sound extreme, but it's a common attitude even if we don't back it up with violence or intimidation. Know this, what we "put out" in the natural can be very different than what we "put out" in the spiritual. When we have to control everything, we put out a spirit of intimidation on a spiritual level, and it's received by our spouses and children. I know this from experience. I had never been violent, but my wife was intimidated by me and my kids seemed to be afraid of me. I didn't know why. Then a spirit of intimidation was cast out of me and I realized things can be very different in the natural than in the spiritual.

We will try to control our children when we live in fear. We will tell them where they can and can't go. We will tell them what to wear and what time to be home. We will constantly call them to check up on them. We will control their behavior in public and make sure they are seen as "perfect" little children. We control everything they watch and say. When they are old enough to date, we will try to control who they go out with and who they spend time with. Things tend to get pretty ugly at that point. We control their schools and jobs. If they are doing anything we have deemed inappropriate, we let them know. As I said before, there is wisdom in setting godly boundaries and guidelines, but there is sin in refusing to totally release and entrust them to the Lord. We need to set those godly boundaries and pray God would conform our children's hearts to his own. We are not our children's protectors, God is. When we are controlled by fear we don't just think it's okay to worry about our kids, we think it's our job. I have heard many people say, "It's my job to worry about my kids. I'm a mother." That may seem honorable, but it's sinful. When we think that way, what we are saying is that we can do it better than God. Fear blinds us to this truth. Not only do we not see this as sin, but we have justified it.

We have to control our jobs when we are in fear. Perfectionism is fear-based. We have to be the best because we can't fail. We must do everything our way and only our way because it's the best way. We think that if someone does it better they are better than us. Fear will keep us from doing things other people's way even when we know their way is better. Fear will drive us to the top of our fields while everything else in our lives falls apart.

We control our homes out of fear. How many times have we cleaned the house before guests come over? It's not wrong to have a clean home, but what's the motivation for cleaning? Many times it's to let our guests know that we are clean and good people. We fear what people may think about us if our homes are a mess. Fear motivates how clean our homes are, how big our homes are, and what we put in them. We fear man's disapproval, so we strive to make everyone approve us.

Yes, we even try to control God out of fear. I say try because unlike the other things in our lives, it's impossible to manipulate or control God. As believers we know we can't control God, but that doesn't stop us from trying. How often do we fast, have quiet time, pray, read the Bible, or go to church in order to get God on our side? Many times it's only when things get really bad that we turn to religious activities to try to illicit an intervention from God. Very few people would admit this, but many of us do it. Fear is completely irrational.

Why do we hold on so tight? Because fear has convinced us that if we aren't in control, everything around us is going to fall apart. Fear tells us we need control in order to prevent bad things from happening. We hold on so tightly because when there is an inability to know or understand the perfect love of God, our acceptance, validation, and worth (essentially our love) comes from these things I have mentioned. If these things should fall away, so does our acceptance, validation, and worth.

Why in the world wouldn't we try to control everything when our sense of love is found in them?

Fear blocks our ability to have an intimate relationship with God because, like I said before, fear is the opposite of faith and without faith it's impossible to please God. The most important assignment of fear is to wreck our relationship with our Daddy, God.

How Does Fear Affect My Marriage?

Have you ever tried to be around someone who worries constantly for an extended period of time? Many of you are saying, "Yeah, I am married to that someone." It gets old. It has sucked all of the peace out of your house, right? It is very hard for one person in a marriage relationship to live in peace when the other is in constant fear. You can see what I am getting at here. Throw in the control issues and we can see how this situation is bound to cause some discord in our marriages.

Worrying about the finances is a big one. We live in fear of money so often, which is a little strange because most of us love money. Kara used to tell me that she would have no peace about our finances because she knew that I had no peace about our finances. We really could not even have a peaceful conversation about the finances because anytime it was mentioned the anxiety level went through the roof because we were both worrying about it so much. That caused our irritability to rise, and it was just a mess.

Money has been credited with the demise of a large portion of marriages. There are many issues that rise between spouses that have to do with money, and most of them have a root in fear.

The fear of man is made up of the fear of abandonment, failure, and rejection. These three fears really hurt our marriage relationships. We tend to have the most fear of the people we love the most. It's those people who have the ability to hurt us the most. Usually those people are our spouses.

The fear of abandonment keeps us strapped to our spouse's side. We always have to know where they are going and when they will be back. Kara shared earlier about how she was a very "needy" person. Wherever I was, she had to be also. It went far beyond her enjoying my company and had become a real need in her life. She had a desperate fear of being abandoned and having to live alone. This is very annoying to our spouses, trust me, because it results in smothering behavior. Bitterness and resentment can be byproducts of the fear of abandonment.

The fear of failure will drive us to be the best in every area of our existence. The problem is that being the best in one area typically means we are falling short in another. The fear of failure keeps us at our jobs late striving to be the best employee in the company while our spouses are at home alone wondering why we would rather be at work than at home with them. Many times as our work life flourishes our family life wilts. If we direct our attention on our failing families, our work suffers. If we turn our attention to our work, our families suffer. Fear does not allow balance. It's all or nothing. Fear of failure makes us bitter competitors, as winning is the only acceptable outcome. The fear of failure will keep us striving to be the perfect wife or husband, mother or father, son or daughter, provider, employee, housekeeper, and so on. Essentially, the fear of failure will keep us striving to be perfect. Of course that can never happen, so we live our lives unsatisfied and in constant irritation.

Finally, the fear of rejection keeps us inside ourselves. We refuse to be vulnerable with our spouses because we think they will reject what they see. We perceive emotional people are weak and rejected. We learn this because many times over the course of our lives we have been hammered with rejection when we risked being emotional and vulnerable. Fear of rejection blocks our ability to intimately connect with our spouses because we are terrified they will laugh or tell us we're not who they thought we were. We fear rejection because it makes us feel like crap. It hurts to feel rejected, so we take precautions to make sure it doesn't happen to us.

I was a very fearful person. Fear of man was running my life. As a result, I was a very controlling person. I almost never gave up control to my wife because a part of my identity was found in being the one who holds things together or knows the right answers. Any perceived situation where I wasn't in control was a threat to me. Nobody could do things the right way except for me. When things went wrong or I made a mistake, it was never my fault. I always blamed someone else. This only bred resentment and bitterness in my wife. Not helpful for our relationship. I tried to find many different ways to show Kara that I loved and appreciated her. It was always superficial. We can give our spouses all the gifts and acts of service that we want, but if the giving does not come from a place of substance within ourselves, it is easily spotted. Fear will drive us to give our spouses what they don't really need and prevent us from giving them what they do need. We are aware there is a problem but don't know how to change things.

We were not meant to live in fear. I have a friend who, over the last two years, has lost a million-dollar business. He came in for ministry, and as the appointment progressed, admitted that he was afraid that if he lost his house he would be a failure and his wife would leave him. Now this person had already lost most everything else, but he saw the house as the last straw. There was nothing that this person could do to earn money. He could not find a job anywhere. There was no available work in his field. Imagine the torment of fearing that the loss of his house would mean the loss of his family and there being nothing he could do to stop it. Do you think that made life easy at home? He had to face his wife every day feeling like a failure and living with the fear that she might not stick around. Praise God that today this person is walking free from fear, and God has started to restore some things back to his family as he has grown closer to God.

Fear of rejection, failure, and abandonment will work together to bring in the fear of conflict. This is particularly dangerous because when we are afraid of conflict, we do not face issues that need to be faced. We do not admit hurt and pain, and we brush things away. We say, "What happened happened, and we do not need to talk about it anymore." Just because we do not deal with issues does not mean that they go away. They just get pushed down. I know that there are many of us who have been married for years and we have years' worth of hurt pushed down inside of us. We are going to talk about that more in the next chapter.

Fear suffocates our marriages. It keeps us from talking about concerns about our marriages and the things affecting them. Fear drives us apart.

Dealing with fear has allowed Kara and me to move into deeper relationship with each other. We do not live in fear anymore. We don't worry about finances, and we try our best to resist the temptation to control. We know that God will provide for us. It was not always like that. Yes, there are times when we still get attacked by worry. I would be in error to tell you that once you deal with bondage you never have to deal with attacks again. However, with the awareness and knowledge of who to fight and how to fight, the attacks can and will be deflected. The great thing is that when you move from fear to faith, you will get blessed. We have all that we need. We have made sacrifices as the Lord has instructed us, but we have all that we need.

The person that I mentioned earlier who was afraid of losing his house is walking in a deeper, more passionate relationship with God since dealing with fear. His wife is also dealing with her fears, and they are enjoying so much more peace in their marriage than they ever have.

* * *

From Kara:

As a young child of about five, my family and I went to a water park. I came down the slide first and for some reason got mixed up and wandered off. Before I knew it, I was lost. I was completely terrified and literally felt sick to my stomach. Finally, after what seemed like hours, a lifeguard approached me and helped me find my family. In all reality, it was my fault that I got lost—I didn't follow directions like I was supposed to. But in my mind the experience justified the fear of being abandoned.

I believe that most of the time, fear is passed down generationally through the different avenues Jesse mentioned and that most of us have been exposed to it in some way. Events in our lives, like what happened to me, simply reinforce and deepen what is already there. On some level, I feel that I dealt with the three "biggies" that Jesse mentioned. Fear of being abandoned and fear of rejection were the primary fears that I struggled with. Jesse and I have already mentioned my neediness, which was a manifestation of the fear of being abandoned and also of the fear of rejection. I can also remember the ways in which I subconsciously tried to control my children. As many parents do, I would say things like, "Don't get too close to the pool or you will fall in and drown." The Bible warns many times about the power that our words have: "The tongue has the power of life and death, and those who love it will eat its fruit" (Proverbs 18:21).

I now try instead to say things like "Don't get too close to the pool because it's not very safe." I used this same type of control with Jesse. Ultimately, I knew at the time that Jesse was in control, but I would still try my best. Like Jesse, my biggest fear in marriage was that he would cheat on me. In my attempts to control, I would constantly call him when he was away, talk badly about attractive women, try to fulfill all of his needs, etc.

Since putting my absolute trust in God and walking out of

these fears, I recognize the things that I truly have no control over. I simply give them over to God and trust that he will take care of me. My relationship with Jesse since then has been so much freer in the way that we are now able to interact with each other. I can now approach Jesse to discuss finances without the thought that it will bring torment into our home. I also do not fear for my children's safety, as I know that God is their protector. Jesse now has the freedom to do what he needs without worrying that I will be checking up on him regularly.

* * *

Fear, just like the unloving, is a block to the marriage that we desire. We just cannot get there with fear in the way.

Bitterness

The most intense and serious spiritual warfare that I have had has been with bitterness. Most of those serious battles came in the months following that night my wife revealed that there had been unfaithfulness. So I have had run-ins with bitterness in myself and many times in ministry with others. It is a nasty spirit, and it is the most violent spirit.

What Is It?

For I see that you are full of bitterness and captive to sin.

Act 8:23

First of all, bitterness is a spirit. Peter is talking in this passage to Simon the sorcerer. Simon has just asked Peter to give him the power to give the Holy Spirit to anyone that he wants to. He is being rebuked by Peter here. Peter says that he is full of bitterness and therefore captive to sin. At this point, I take us back to Romans where Paul talks about sin being an entity. Paul talks about the body of sin that is alive within him. We talked about this in chapter eleven. So if we are captive to sin, then we are captive to an entity or being.

This takes us easily into the next point, which is that bitterness is sin. We are commanded to put bitterness away. We are commanded to have nothing to do with bitterness.

> Let all bitterness, and wrath, and anger, and clamour, and evil speaking, be put away from you, with all malice:
>
> Ephesians 4:31

> Looking diligently lest any man fail of the grace of God; lest any root of bitterness springing up trouble you, and thereby many be defiled;
>
> Hebrews 12:15

The original Greek word for bitterness is *pikria,* meaning poison. **Bitterness is poison**! Bitterness will rot our souls and kill us from the inside out. We will get into this a little more later on, but we have seen bitterness as the root of many diseases and illnesses.

Bitterness is similar to the unloving in that bitterness has subcategories to it. Bitterness follows a progression and always tries to funnel us toward the most extreme, which is murder. When a person commits murder, he/she did not get to that extreme in a short amount of time. That person went through the progression of bitterness and found himself or herself at the extreme. To murder is to not be in control of our own bodies anymore and is to be completely subject to the enemy. When it gets to that, we are no longer dealing with a person but a demon that has been given extreme rights to our behavior.

The progression is as follows:

- Unforgiveness

- Bitterness
- Resentment
- Anger
- Retaliation
- Wrath
- Violence
- Hatred
- Murder

I know that there are serious wounds that would make it seem like a person could go from unforgiveness to murder in a matter of minutes. I felt like it could be possible for me to go there that night the bomb dropped on me.

In the months that followed Kara's unfaithfulness, I experienced multiple times bitterness getting a foothold in me and starting to take me down that progression. I could get a certain way down that progression fairly easily because the wound was so fresh, but I never got to murder. The thought may have crossed my mind, but I never felt I was in danger of committing to it. I was able to reject the thought very quickly. I believe the reason I was able to do that is because I do not walk in bitterness. I try my best to walk in forgiveness. I used to walk in a certain degree of bitterness, but God delivered me from its grasp through ministry. That was before the incident, thank goodness.

Where Does It Come From?

This section is not going to be very long because the roots of bitterness are almost the same as the last two. If a person has an angry and unforgiving mother or father, chances are that the person is going to be angry and bitter because they were born into that bondage.

There is a root or avenue of bitterness that is different from the rest. That avenue is unforgiveness. When we do not forgive, we give bitterness a right to come into our lives and torment us. I am sure that we could all think of a person that we know who seems, to you, to be a very angry and bitter person. Now consider if that person seems to have a lot of trouble forgiving people. Maybe you do not know if that person has trouble forgiving. Maybe you do. I will tell you it is a fact that if a person is walking in bitterness, he or she also is walking in unforgiveness. They go together. We cannot have one without the other.

Do you think that Jesus took this subject seriously? You bet he did. Jesus knows how dangerous and devastating it is to walk under the control of bitterness.

> But if ye forgive not men their trespasses, neither will your Father forgive your trespasses.
>
> Matthew 6:15

This verse is repeated in Mark 11:26. Do you think that Jesus wanted us to pay attention to this? This is an ultimatum. God is saying either choose to forgive or we ourselves will not be forgiven. Why is this so important to God? God never says that unless we love each other he will not love us. God is trying to prevent us from going down the progression of bitterness. God laid the groundwork, being this passage, in order to serve as a serious deterrent to walking in unforgiveness. God knows what bitterness does to us physically, spiritually, and emotionally. The most important of those being the damage that bitterness does spiritually. Jesus made a statement of tough love.

I am going to share a story with you about bitterness and an avenue it can come in through. This is important because it will show you that bitterness can come from intangible avenues as well. I had owned a pool service business for two years. I was so tired of it. One of my greatest desires was to someday own a business, and God made that happen for me. Two years later I was trying to sell it. I was tired of the headache and the hassle. I was tired of the phone calls and pretty much anything that had to do with the business.

It was a Wednesday, and I had just gotten back into town the day before from my anniversary vacation with my wife. I had to go clean pools. I was particularly irritable and just sicker of the business than I had ever been. I was upset and bitter that day. I just did not want to be doing what I was doing and … well … you get the idea.

I was just about done for the day, and my attitude had not improved. All of a sudden my right heel began to hurt. Every time I stepped down on it, it shot pain through my whole right foot. I am sure you all know how it feels when something on your body is swollen, and that is how my foot felt, but the strange thing was I could not see any swelling. It was so painful it reduced me to a limp for the better part of two weeks.

I started to ask some questions about what I was experiencing in my foot and found out I had what seemed to be plantar fasciitis. This condition is incurable. There is only treatment. The treatment is steroid injections into the foot and then crutches following the procedure for a couple of weeks. After all of that, there is no guarantee it won't come back; in fact, it commonly does come back again.

Well, I quickly decided that wasn't going to be an option for me. Instead I wrote to a ministry who has been dealing with the spiritual roots of diseases for twenty years and asked them what the possible roots to this affliction were. One of the roots is bitterness. At first I dismissed this because there was no one I knew of that I was holding bitterness toward. A couple of days later, the Lord brought this back to my mind and brought a picture of the pool service business. The Lord spoke and said that I was holding bitterness against the business. It was like a lightbulb went on in my head. That night I confessed the bitterness that I was holding toward the business and commanded that any spirit of bitterness leave. The next day I woke up with only slight pain. Keep in mind that the previous day I was still limping around. Later on that same day, the pain was completely gone, and it has never been back.

That is a powerful testimony of what bitterness can do to us if we give it the rights to, and also the kind of freedom we get through Jesus and the healing that comes with it. It also shows us that bitterness can have an avenue through intangible things like work, school, etc.

What Does It Do?

Simply put, *bitterness is a poison* that, immediately after we decide to hold on to it, starts to kill us from the inside out. It does not just stop with us though. As it is killing us, it destroys our relationships and especially our marriages.

I have begun to see many outward expressions as being a result of a more deeply rooted problem. Or, on the flip side, many outward expressions as being a result of deep spiritual and emotional healing.

Bitterness will cause explosions of rage. I remember that I really had to deal with bitterness as it related to my dogs. I was bitter toward my dog because of the gross amount of peeing and pooping she did inside my house. This is not funny, people. I would almost lose control of my actions. Chairs would get pushed and even thrown, and, sadly, so would the dog. Yeah, it was a problem. See, the chairs and dogs being thrown around were an outward response to a deeper-rooted problem.

Bitterness can also cause disease much in the same way that fear and the unloving do. Some of the diseases that have been linked to bitterness are arthritis, high cholesterol, nosebleeds, heart attacks, and Meniere's disease. Oh, and plantar fasciitis.

Bitterness will age your body as well. I was in ministry with a young man in his early twenties and he looked like he was in his forties. Over the time that we had with him, God began to speak into the bitterness that he was holding on to. The next week when he came back, he looked like he had found the fountain of youth. It was amazing. He looked younger and felt younger. Praise God.

Bitterness hinders our relationship with God. That makes sense, right? If we have bitterness, we are walking in unforgiveness, and that is a sin. Sin severely hampers our relationship with God. Also, many of us are bitter at God himself. Yeah, I would say that would hinder our relationship with God.

Bitterness destroys relationships with people. Is it much fun to be around angry people? I don't think so. Walking on eggshells so you don't do something to set them off is not my favorite way of passing time. We never know what is going to set them off, do we? It could be anything.

Bitterness destroys our relationships with our kids. Understand that if there is a stronghold of bitterness in you, you do not necessarily have to have a reason to be angry, you just are. Bitterness will make your children afraid of you. It comes out when you speak to them, discipline them, and have any interaction with them. We have heard and been taught that it is good for kids to be a little afraid of their fathers. That is not what the Bible teaches. Do you want to be the vessel fear uses to gain rights to your child? I don't.

Bitterness destroys marriages. Imagine being married to that angry person. Some of us don't have to imagine, do we? Bitterness will reduce communication between spouses to one or two word answers. Bitterness will make you afraid of your spouse, and bitterness will make you feel like you are married to a stranger, a stranger who is a ticking time bomb. That takes us into the next question.

How Does Bitterness Affect My Marriage?

Bitterness will suck the life right out of a marriage. Bitterness will not allow us to fight fairly with our spouses. Bitterness will remind us of all the hurt and pain our spouses have caused us over the years and bring it out in future conflicts. You might not get hit with direct mentions of past hurt, but you will get hit with the emotions of past hurts.

Most of us carry the stronghold of bitterness into our marriages. Let us set aside, for a moment, any problem, hurt, or pain your spouse has caused you and talk about what bitterness does to our marriages when we carry it with us to the altar.

The stronghold of bitterness makes us irritable. We find that there are things our spouses do that just irritate and annoy us. Most of these things are not a big deal in and of themselves, but the stronghold of bitterness amplifies everything one hundred times. We are just irritable people. We do not like to asked personal questions, and it irritates us when someone does. You can see how that would be a problem in a marriage. We think, *What right does he/she have to ask me this stuff? This is my business, and she/he is so nosy.*

We bring irritations from the day back home and take them out on our families. We tend not to enjoy people very much. There are many firefighters and cops with bitterness issues. It is not uncommon to hear one of these people say, "I just hate people." I used to say that. We are set off by the smallest, most insignificant things. Those small annoyances from our spouses are enough to bring us to yelling and screaming given the right circumstances.

We are not enjoyable to be around because of the anger we carry with us everywhere we go. We hold on to resentment, and not very often do we have nice things to say about anyone. We seem to be confrontational much of the time and are not too concerned about other people's feelings.

Being that we do not tend to like people very much, conversations with our spouses are extremely limited in nature and sometimes seem strained. We do not want to have to explain ourselves and do not want to answer to anyone. We judge everyone, especially our spouses.

We are impatient and harsh with our children. We get angry that they demand our time, so we tend not to spend as much time with them as we should.

So now let's bring into the mix any offenses, past or recurring, that we are holding against our spouses. I have found that many times we start harboring bitterness against our spouses without even realizing it.

I was in an appointment with a young man who had been married for a couple of years. He was experiencing some hard times in his marriage. I asked him if he needed to forgive his wife for anything. He said no and that it was not a problem. I said okay, and we continued to talk. Over the next hour or so, we discussed a handful of things that would have created resentment and bitterness against his spouse in any normal human being. There were some very hurtful things that had happened to this young man. Every time I asked him how he responded to those situations, he told me that he brushed it off and that it doesn't bother him. What he did tell me, though, is that he wanted to be able to stop "blowing up" at his wife over the dumbest things. He told me that little fights quickly escalated to large fights and that they were over stupid things. He told me that the smallest thing would set him off. What was happening here was that he was seeing fruit come to the surface from roots of bitterness running deep within him.

Listen, just because we push down hurt and pain and refuse to deal with them doesn't mean it goes away. The response to that statement is typically "Yeah, I know." Ironically, the majority of us who would say "I know" are continually pushing down hurt and pain whether we realize it or not. Here is a little bubble buster: just because you have pushed away pain and hurt, ignoring them for so long that they don't *feel* like hurt or pain anymore, doesn't mean you have dealt with the issues. I know there are many people who believe we should just move on from past hurts and not keep bringing up old pain. Here is something I have found to be true in my life. We will never just move on from hurt and pain unless we acknowledge it, forgive, release judgments, get rid of the spirit of bitterness, and ask for forgiveness for anything we have done wrong. If we do not do those things, then that hurt and pain will come out in one way or another. Maybe not right away, but eventually it will come back again by way of deteriorating relationships, disease, or other hardships.

I allowed myself to feel every single bit of pain and suffering after my wife hurt me. We talked about every emotion I felt. We talked through nights of agony, and we talked about the joy when it came. My wife was and is a vital part of the healing process. There were some that could not understand why we would continue to talk about what happened because it was so painful. Why did we continue to talk about it? Because that's the only way healing can happen. Being willing to acknowledge the hurt and pain and not shutting those feelings out allows God to cleanse and completely heal us. I shudder when I think about what my marriage and life would be like if I had the attitude of "just moving on." I would be an absolute disaster. God is good.

Anyway, the young man listened to me explain a couple of things as to why he might be having a problem with "exploding" over nothing. God spoke to him that night, and he came to the conclusion that there were lots of things he was holding against his wife.

There are many of us that are holding many things toward our spouses that have caused us to become angry at them most of the time. One woman I was ministering to said, "I am just angry at my husband all the time, and I don't know why." It is because of bitterness. It's because of unforgiveness. Remember this. If you have a fruit, you have a root. You may say, "Well, I have forgiven my spouse for ... but I still feel angry at him/her much of the time." It sounds like there is still a root. Many times people speak out forgiveness. I have seen this in ministry. People will make the choice to forgive, and then the complete freedom comes when the spirit of bitterness is commanded to leave. Many times if you speak out forgiveness but then the spirit is never commanded to leave, it stays and continues to hold you in bondage. I have also heard people say, "I will forgive him/her when I'm not angry anymore." ***Beloved, we will*** *never learn to walk in forgiveness until we learn how to forgive in the midst of our pain and anger.* If we wait until the anger is gone, it's most likely been pushed down and hasn't been dealt with. In the midst of anger, we make a choice with our minds, wills, and emotions to call on the supernatural strength and grace of God. True forgiveness is a supernatural act. It is impossible for us to truly forgive on our own. We need a supernatural God to help us complete a supernatural act.

Bitterness is also what motivates us to say things like "Why do I even bother?" Or how about "He/she is just never going to change. I am done! Just do whatever you want to do; I don't even care!"? There is much bitterness and resentment in these statements. Don't get me wrong, I know how frustrating and exhausting it is to feel like our spouses are not listening to us. I have asked my wife to put the car keys into the basket we have designated for keys whenever she gets home. Guess where they would always be? In her purse. Guess what happened more than a couple of times? She would go somewhere in our other car and end up having both sets of keys with her. I was stranded at home a couple of times because of this.

It hurt my feelings because I felt that she did not care about what I wanted. Every time I found the keys in her purse, it said to me, "Jesse, I know you want me to put the keys in the basket, but I don't care about what you want or say." That hurt, and it bred resentment and bitterness. As time went on, my response to finding the keys in her purse escalated more and more. Resentment built on resentment. It didn't matter to me that in reality she was not dismissing my feelings and she did try hard to remember but that isn't the message I received. The problem with resentment is that it's seldom confined to a specific event or circumstance. It has a habit of spilling over into other areas of our marriages. It is like an infection that starts in one body system and then, left untreated, becomes a systemic problem.

Suddenly little annoyances throughout the day elicit an elevated response, especially annoyances that have to do with our spouses. Then we find ourselves in front of a marriage counselor explaining to him or her about how all we do anymore is fight.

For years of my marriage, I walked around irritable much of the time. I did not like it when Kara asked me questions, and I would call her nosy. There were a lot of things she did that irritated me, and I let her know about them all. I knew something was wrong. I wanted to be able to not be irritated when she asked me questions. I wanted to be a whole lot nicer, but I had such a hard time doing that. I thought there was something wrong with me. It was hurting my marriage. We were not connecting intimately because of this issue along with her issues. I wanted to change, but I didn't know how.

Walking through healing for the stronghold of bitterness is what did it for me. God broke that stronghold in me in a ministry appointment, and I began to change. I began to welcome Kara's questions and actually enjoyed answering them. I began to be able to communicate intimately and actually enjoyed doing it. It was a complete transformation.

Maybe you have wondered why it is so easy to remember past hurts and pain your spouse caused you when you are engaged in a conflict with them. Maybe you have not wondered that until just now. Think about it. When your spouse has just done something that has made or is making you so angry, how easy is it to remember what your spouse has done to you in the past? How much more angry do those memories make you?

Beloved, we are in a battle not with ourselves or our spouses but with a very real and powerful enemy. Those memories of past hurts and pains did not just happen to come to you in an angry moment; they were put there by a spirit that ultimately wants to see you and your marriage destroyed. Now let me just clarify that the power the enemy has pales in comparison to the power we have over the enemy through Christ Jesus, but the enemy does have power. If we do not recognize that, we are already defeated.

How many times has the stronghold of bitterness landed married couples in counseling? How many times has the stronghold of bitterness motivated us to cheat on our spouses? "Well, he/she is not paying attention to me, so I will find someone who will." Beloved, bitterness is motivating that thinking, and it is not of you but it is of the world, so put it back where it belongs. How many marriages has the enemy been allowed to destroy? *Fifty to sixty* percent of marriages end in divorce. *Eighty* percent of married couples will experience unfaithfulness. Most married couples cannot connect intimately. Many of us are lashing out at our spouses and we don't know why. Most of us are unhappy in our marriages and we don't know why. We have been taken captive by the kingdom of Satan and we don't even know it.

When will we finally begin to realize that the problem is not us but it is attached to us and there is something we can do about it? When will we finally stop trying to fix our marriages by following a step-by-step solution that only deals with superficial fruit of more deeply rooted bondage and go right to the source and say, "*Jesus! Deliver me from captivity!*"? Beloved, when will we stop talking and singing about freedom and actually experience and witness it in our lives and relationships? When will we say that enough is enough? We are tired of living in fear, we are tired of living in self-hate, and we are tired of living in bitterness and unforgiveness. We are tired of these things interfering in our marriages and relationships. When will we stop blaming everyone else for our problems and take responsibility for all the ways we have hurt and wounded the people we love? When will we step out of self-pity and forcefully advance the Kingdom of God?

Are you ready to release everything that you have been holding against your spouse? Are you desperate for the type of marriage you know God wants you to have? Are you ready to admit that it is impossible to reflect all of who God is to your spouse when you are in bondage to bitterness, fear, and the unloving? It goes beyond your spouse. You cannot get rid of bitterness by forgiving your spouse but not forgiving the person who sexually abused you when you were just a child or the kid that made fun of you in school so much that you still remember their name. It is a package deal. Either you forgive every single person who hurt you or you don't forgive any of them. Bitterness is given a right to stay with you if there is any unforgiveness in you at all. Are you ready to be free? Are you ready to be the husband or wife God has called you to be? Beyond that, are you ready to be the son or daughter God has called you to be?

I want to share a story with you I hope will give you an idea of just how real the spirit of bitterness is. I shared before that I have had some pretty intense battles with bitterness. Probably, to no surprise to you, these battles occurred after my wife revealed what had happened. Over the course of a couple of months, I had to be delivered of the spirit of bitterness six times. The sequence seemed to be that bitterness would be cast out, I would be okay for a while, I would get attacked and allow the enemy to take me down a bad road, and as a result bitterness would wrap its tentacles around me. It would gain access to me seemingly very easily, and that was concerning to me. I did not know what was giving it a right to come back so quickly.

One night I was in the shower, and the enemy started to attack my mind. It led me to start asking my wife questions about what happened, and that is never a good idea. Before I knew it, I felt the presence of bitterness within me. I was sitting on our bed with my arms crossed. Kara had been exposed to this a couple of times before, so she began to pray for me. She took authority over the spirit of bitterness, but I was not ready to let go of it, so it stayed with me. I felt the increasing rage coming, and my whole body began to get hot. I knew what I had to do, but I was being disobedient and rebellious.

I could feel the darkness closing in around me. I felt the familiar pull to just let the bitterness take over and to give it control of me. It is tempting to do that when you are in the middle of a battle. At that moment I heard God speak, and the Lord told me stand up and fight. God showed me a picture of a sword and told me to take it and use it against the enemy. The Lord then showed me a picture of the spirit of bitterness. I will describe it the best that I can. It was a mass of tentacles with darkness in the middle. The darkness in the middle had a twisted and deformed face. It was an ugly and menacing-looking being. The Lord spoke to me again and told me that he has given me the strength to fight so get up and fight. The Lord told me not to let the enemy suck me in. He told me not to give up.

It was at that moment that I decided to fight, so I got on my hands and knees looked at Kara and started, "I choose to forgive…" The past couple of times I had dealt with bitterness, it was at this point that I could feel it in me. This time was no different. As soon as I said those words, I felt a tightening in my stomach. I felt a bubbling or an intense strain inside of me that was rising from my stomach and up into my chest. The strain made me open my mouth and caused me to bear down. If you know what it is like to scream silently with your mouth open, this is what I was experiencing. When I was able to regain my breath, I finished saying, "I forgive you, Kara." At that point I experienced another involuntary silent scream. I was then able to relax.

Then I heard the Lord speak to me and tell me that it was not over. In the past times after I forgave Kara again, that was the end of it. I could feel that God was taking me to a place of total freedom so that I would not have to do this again. I was led to tell Kara that I release her from my condemnation. As soon as I finished that sentence with the word *condemnation,* I experienced something that I have never experienced before. Right after or even as I was finishing that word, I heard a loud and terrible voice in my head scream, "*Oh no you don't!*"

At that moment, my head was jerked so that Kara was in my view, and my eyes involuntarily met hers. I was trying to look away from her, but it did not seem like I was in control. All of a sudden, I saw Kara pushed away from me, and I was sucked backwards. Now Kara and I did not get physically pushed, but what I saw with my eyes was Kara projected farther away from me, and I felt myself get sucked backward. I have been in ministry appointments with people when the spirits take control, so I know what it looks like, but I had never felt it before. I am convinced that for a couple of seconds Kara was no longer dealing with me but that she was dealing with a demon manifesting through me.

This only lasted a couple of seconds because I was able to get my bearings and regain control. It just took a second for everything to fall back into normal view as far as my eyes were concerned. I looked at Kara to see a look of absolute terror on her face. Kara was getting a crash course in dealing with the demonic, and unfortunately, it was through me.

Things began to settle down a little bit, but I still heard the Lord say to me, "It's not over yet." I could feel that the spirit that had spoken to me had settled down. I could barely feel it in me at this point, but I knew it was still there and had to be dealt with. I sensed that this was a very important battle and that I needed to push through. I really had no idea or sense of leading what to do next, so I just started to repeat the line that seemed to really agitate the demon. I started to repeat, "Kara, I release you from my condemnation and judgment." It was not very long before I felt that spirit start to strain and well up within the pit of my stomach again.

Poor Kara! She was still sitting on the bed with a look of shock and concern on her face. She did not know what to do. I think she was still praying. I was in agony and writhing on the bed as the Lord spoke to me and said, "Deal with the rights." A couple of weeks prior to this the Lord spoke to me one night about the rights that I was holding on to. The right to hold Kara in condemnation, the right to hurt her like she hurt me, the right to hold on to unforgiveness, and the biggest one was the right to hate her. You can see how it would be impossible for me, or anyone, to keep the door shut on bitterness while hanging on to these rights. No wonder why it seemed so easy for bitterness to capture me.

So I started to come out of agreement with these rights,

and there was a whirlwind of response. As I was speaking, I was also straining and silently screaming, and the spirit of bitterness was being expelled. It was exhausting. When I got to the "right to hate her," it produced the biggest and most intense response thus far. I spoke out the words, and as soon as I did, I was jerked forward facedown onto the bed and started to hack and choke violently, followed by a series of dry heaves. I was sure that I was going to vomit all over the bed, but the only thing that was coming out was the spirit. This was followed by about three or four loud and involuntary wails as most of my strength left me, and it was over.

I was sobbing loudly on the bed at that point as snot was pouring out of my nose, a lovely picture I know. The emotional release was incredible, and the joy that followed was unparalleled by anything I have ever experienced. Kara began to relax and come back down the wall a little and was crying with me.

God set me free from the bondage of bitterness that night, and since that night, I have not been captured by bitterness. Oh, there are still times when I feel the attack of bitterness relating to what happened, but I resist it and am no longer in bondage to it. Praise God!

How can we hope or expect to live in peace with our spouses while, at the same time, holding on to the rights to bitterness? Oh, I am sure that there are lots of times where there is peace in your marriage, but the times when the fruit of bitterness rears its head seem to overshadow those times of peace and will eventually make you wonder if you have ever experienced peace in your marriage.

As I reflected back over my marriage before God brought healing, it was so hard for me to remember times when I was not angry. The truth is that most of the time I was not angry. However, the times that I was angry and irritable seem to be the only times I was able to recall, so my opinion of how my marriage used to be was not good at all. This is a scheme from the enemy, and accusation plays a part in this one. The problem was that believing that I spent most of my time being irritable and angry was what caused me to hate the way my marriage used to be and consequently hate the way that I used to be. That is problematic because all that does is bring more bitterness and resentment toward the old marriage and myself.

* * *

From Kara:

Bitterness, for me, did not manifest in outward displays of rage, like it did for Jesse. I was the type of person who repressed and buried my anger. When someone did something that hurt or angered me, I would say that I forgave them, and maybe I did, but the root was never truly dealt with. It always came back and then intensified the inward emotions with repeat offenses. I was left feeling like a victim. Because I was always burying my hurts and anger, I never felt like things were truly dealt with, probably because they weren't. I had the attitude that people were always doing things to hurt me and that I pretty much had it together. I became a doormat because I did not want to confront the issues that were there. It wasn't until I dealt with the roots in me that I was able to confront issues in a godly way and truly had the ability to forgive by separating the sin from the person. The outcome of this in my marriage was a more balanced relationship to where Jesse and I began to share annoyances and frustrations without allowing bitterness to interfere in any way. Issues are now more easily resolved with love instead of accusation and anger.

On the other side of things, I would like to talk a little bit about how Jesse's bitterness affected me. Have you ever felt like you needed to walk on eggshells around someone? If you have, then you probably know someone who is outwardly bitter. For someone, like myself, who doesn't (or didn't, in my case) like conflict, these people tap into the fear inside of others. Jesse talked a little about the car keys situation. During this time, I still was dealing with the fear of man, so any time I would forget to put the car keys back, I became extremely fearful. In reality, this seems silly because Jesse never once laid a hand on me. It was the bitterness inside of him that was intimidating the fear inside of me. Jesse still prefers that the car keys be put in the right place, understandably so. Now, in this same situation, I am not afraid of Jesse when I forget, as I still sometimes do. I simply apologize from my heart, and he forgives me. It's really that easy! How incredibly freeing it was when I realized that I didn't need to be afraid of the husband who loves me so deeply!

* * *

Bitterness is a destructive spirit that has the ability, if we give it the rights, to poison us, our relationships, and most importantly our walk with God. Make no mistake about it. If you give any of these three spirits a right to be in your life, they are going to be there, and they do not respect anything about you. They will kick you when you are high and kick you when you are low. They are out for one purpose and one purpose only. That is to destroy you and take as many people down with you as they can. Let's stop being that vessel, shall we.

We are not called to live in bondage. Hebrews 2:13–15 talks about our trust in God that he is able to deliver us from bondage to the fear of death. Romans 8:15 and 21 talks about how we have not received, and can be delivered from, the bondage of fear and corruption. I suppose that we can lump in all sin with the bondage of corruption. So let's get delivered and allow God to transform us and then allow him to transform our lives.

?

Let's Get Free!

I have said before that my hope and prayer is God uses everything in this book to give you insight and revelation into your own life. I pray these things have been revelatory to you. Maybe God has directed a light into your mind and spirit and shown you ways you have been a victim to the enemy.

Maybe there is some hope that is starting to build in you as you continue to read. There is a reason you are the way you are. There is a reason your marriage is struggling, and it's not just because marriage is hard. It is not because there is something wrong with you as a person. It is not because you are not reading the Bible enough or going to church every Sunday and Wednesday night. It isn't because God doesn't care about you and your marriage. It is not because your spouse doesn't love you anymore. You may say to that, "My spouse told me he/she doesn't love me anymore, so how can you say that?" A spouse who would say that has a twisted belief of what love really is, and he/she doesn't understand it because he/she doesn't know it themselves. A spouse who says that to you does not know how to love. That is not his/her fault either. That is a result of their brokenness and wounds running very deep within.

The reason your marriage is struggling is not because you have failed to implement the tools you have learned over a weekend of marriage counseling. I am sure you have tried and even been successful implementing them for a short amount of time. Because of the roots keeping us in bondage, we have no chance of making the tools supposed to make our marriages a success a permanent part of our relationships. If the weekends and seminars that teach tools only are so great, then why do more than half of our marriages end in divorce and 80 percent of them are polluted with unfaithfulness? Come on, people! If the theology of marriage therapy and counseling is doing such a great job, why do born-again Christians make up 27 percent of the divorce rate? Why are born-again Christians making up the second highest divorce rated religious group? Where are the results?

We are not seeing results because the known theology of how we help and fix marriage only treats the symptoms and neglects the disease. I am not trying to undermine, put down, or bash professional therapists and counselors, but a marriage that is half broken is still broken. There are some very gifted and godly therapists, counselors, speakers and teachers. God has given many of them insight and revelation of tools we can use in our marriages that will help us to become what God wants us to become. The problem is tools are only good for people who know how to use them. If the roots of our problems aren't exposed and dealt with, we will have no idea how to use any tools.

I am a paramedic, so let me use a trauma analogy. I am not going to splint a broken leg before I address an arterial bleed. Life-threatening injuries are always addressed first. If I take care of the leg and the patient dies of blood loss, first of all I am in some serious trouble, and second of all I have done much more harm than good. That is what is happening today with the help we seek for our "on the rocks" marriages. Many times we go see someone and get some tools and/or emotional help, and demonic strongholds and possible bondage are not addressed. The result is that we die individually and our marriage falls apart because the roots were never dealt with. The first step to a marriage God desires is to allow him to heal individual emotional pain, which exposes the ways the demonic have been allowed to enter our lives and cause chaos. This will allow us to become the sons and daughters God desires us to be. The main purpose of this is to finally be able to experience a relationship with God. This is far more important than any human relationship.

You may be saying, "I have always desired a more intimate relationship with God. I just can't seem to get there. I have a hard time spending time with him, and it's hard for me to hear him speak. I go to church every Sunday. I fast and read my Bible, but I still feel disconnected. Many times I don't think I know him at all. When I get honest with myself, I have to say I don't have an intimate relationship with God. I'm not experiencing the love he promised." A friend of mine who wrote a book called *This Is Not a Dress Rehearsal* has this to say: "I was finally able to recognize that I had a very hard time hearing the voice of God. One night I asked him why I couldn't hear him. He answered me with 'Because you think you already know everything" (Patricia Rallo). Think about that for a minute.

Let's address transformation.

> Do not conform any longer to the pattern of this world, but be transformed by the renewing of your mind. Then you will be able to test and approve what God's will is—his good, pleasing and perfect will.
>
> Romans 12:2 (NIV)

I have been pondering and processing something for a little while now. People who have been truly transformed can tell there has been a dramatic change in their life, but they are unable to really describe it or explain when it happened. This truth hit me hard as I began to remember thoughts and experiences I have had over the recent years.

Something has changed in me. I can't really describe it or tell anyone when it happened, but I don't feel like the same person I once was. I know for most of my life the phrase "be transformed" was well known, but there was no revelation of emotion or sense of realism that came with it. In short, I had no idea what it meant or even how it felt to be transformed.

As I have been pondering this, I have to say that over the last couple of years I feel I have literally been transformed. I feel like a brand new birth. It's truly unexplainable. It doesn't mean I haven't sinned in the last years or come close to that, but let me try to explain what has happened with a couple of experiences I have had.

I know that sin is sin and God sees all sin as the same; however, we all carry our own scales that say which sin is weightier than another. That's a tough nut to crack. I had my own set of sins that were much worse than others, and though I felt like God had done some significant healing in me to bring me to a place where I could recognize sin as sin, I hadn't really experienced that revelation in a tangible way.

One evening I was meditating on the Lord and just thinking about him and something came to my mind. It was a sin I know would have never registered as something I would need to repent of in the past. It was, in my mind, a little sin and in the past would have never been on my grid for repentance. Not only did the Lord bring this sin to my mind with a sense of repentance, but my heart was *wrecked* because of the sin. My heart was just wounded because of this sin that previously would have never had an effect on me. I remember thinking in that moment, *When did this happen? When did I start feeling this way?* I was aware of enough in that moment to recognize I was not the same person in my heart and soul (mind, will, and emotions) I used to be and I couldn't explain why. To be honest, and this is kind of funny, I felt sort of violated. As if someone snuck in and changed who I was into someone else. Very weird.

Another example is my relationship with my son. Because of my past wounds over the course of my whole life, God has had to unravel some things over the last couple of years in order to break down a perceived block or hindrance so a godly relationship could be established between me and my son. The blocks prevented me from really understanding how to love my son, and over the last couple of years, God has done some amazing things in that. One week recently I suddenly became aware of how much I had been enjoying my son. I just enjoy him and the blocks seem to have vanished. This is a dramatic change that I can feel happened in my heart and soul, and I can't explain it or tell anyone when it happened, but something happened.

It's the same type of change I have experienced in my renewed relationship with Kara. All of a sudden I was enjoying her. I wanted to spend time with her, and I sincerely missed her when I went to work. The whole dynamic of our relationship changed as we were transformed. Suddenly, Kara was seeing God in me and I was seeing God in her. The things I wanted to see God change in my and Kara's relationship was happening naturally as we were, and are, being transformed.

These unexplainable changes occurred without any extra fasting, praying, Bible reading, or church going. I'm not saying these things aren't important; my point is that I haven't been doing anything extra to try to make a change happen. So as I was processing these things, the Lord brought to me Romans 12:2 where Paul says, "Be transformed." Do we understand what this implies?

The Greek word for transformed is *metamorphoo*. It means *changed by something*. It's not something that we can make happen. To be transformed consists of being completely changed by an outside force. What I have experienced for most of my life is the belief in order to experience that inward change or transformation I had to read my Bible more, pray more, have more quiet time, go to church more, and fast more. I had to try my best to be a nice and godly person.

The problem is that the religious things we do have nothing to do with being transformed. It goes back to the fact that we can't transform ourselves. We cannot change our soul. We cannot sanctify our soul. Only God can do these things. I know we have all heard that only God can change us, but the challenge is to evaluate if we live like we believe this.

So the question I ask myself is "If there is nothing we can do to make this change/transformation happen, what is our part?" We have to come to a place of desperation. I recognize two different types of desperation.

The first type is one that says "I can't live one more day in my current circumstances. Circumstances are too much and I need relief." This desperation says "Just help me through this hard time and I will be on my way." The second type is one that says "I can't live one more day without being totally transformed and saturated by the presence of God, and I am willing to give up everything and everything I always thought I knew to get it." This type of desperation goes way beyond circumstances and says "Daddy! Please change everything about me. Change me into who you want me to be because I can't live without you anymore."

I have seen both types in ministry (unfortunately mostly the former), and the latter gets free while the former stays in chains. How do we get to this level of desperation? This level of desperation is only ignited by God in our souls as we cry out, "Father, strip me of everything. I want to become like a child again. I am willing to admit that I don't know anything. Replace everything I thought I knew with truth." We will truly only be able to say these things when relationship with our Daddy becomes more important than everything else and we live like it is. This level of desperation doesn't happen in ministry. It doesn't happen through someone else. It happens when we pursue God one on one. Obedience is the fruit of this level of desperation.

The only thing I can advise you to do is to ask God to give it to you and respond to the tugging on your spirit. There is no formula or step-by-step process. Just ask Father. It is only in desperation that we can see our "blind spots" and invite God in to heal them. It should take a lot of pressure off of us if we believe the only thing we have to do to be transformed is to become desperate. It's not an easy road by any means, but at least we don't have to strive and drive for it.

Allow me to balance a little and bring back the fasting, Bible reading, and quiet time. I have noticed that as I walked the path of being transformed a genuine and sincere thirst began to grow in me to sit in front of God, whatever that looked like. Maybe fasting, maybe quiet time. Whatever. The point is that the feelings of "obligation" unexplainably began to fade. There are, of course, other things along the way, like deliverance, that are critical to the journey, but the key to transformation lies in our level and type of desperation. I can't say it means we won't ever sin again, but what I have experienced is a completely and unexplainably different response to *every* sin and unexplainable changes inside of who I am. It means being truly being born again.

The Word says to be deeply rooted in Christ. In order to achieve this we have to be willing to let God uproot everything that is not godly in our lives and set our roots in him.

I did not go see a professional therapist or family counselor to help me deal with the terrible pain and hurt that my wife caused me. I was not opposed to seeing a professional therapist. What I was opposed to was seeing a professional therapist who did not address the demonic side as well as the emotional. Quite frankly, I do not know of any professional therapists and counselors locally who address both. That does not mean that I did not seek counseling. There were some very important people in my life God used to help me through this. There was a lot that God did just him and me, but there was also a lot that God did through some important people in my life. Isaiah says:

For unto us a child is born, unto us a son is given: and the government shall be upon his shoulder: and his name shall be called Wonderful, Counselor, The mighty God, The everlasting Father, The Prince of Peace.

Isaiah 9:6

Why are we so quick to run to man to hear what man has to say about man's issues? It says right here that my God is Wonderful and a Counselor. He is my everlasting Father and my Prince of Peace. Why do we not go to God first?

Sometimes we think we are doing the right thing because we are reading the Bible or seeing a Christian counselor. Doing these things make us feel that we are going to God first and giving him a chance to work in our lives. I would say you're on the right track but that we need to embrace all of him and not just the things that we are comfortable with.

I wanted God to counsel me through all of the pain and heal my broken heart. When I think about how close God drew me to him over the months following the bomb, it brings tears to my eyes. He was and is my strength. He was and is my peace. He was and is my father. He carried me. He counseled me. He brought revelations of his love for me I never imagined a human could experience. He gave me the courage to fight. He gave me the courage to move forward. He directed my steps, and when it was time to turn the corner and leave the old emotions behind to embrace the new emotions, he gently let me know and led me through that. Understand though that he did this because I was desperate and willing to embrace the truth that there was and is a demonic army waiting to throw me into bondage and captivity. He helped me to understand the tools he has given all of us to allow us to walk free from the enemy.

In just one year Kara and I experienced a level of healing said to take years and years. God helped us to move forward with a much healthier relationship than we had before, and I can honestly say that the grief lasts only for the night. God continues to give me the oil of joy for mourning. It was the hardest year of my life. If you only knew how many times my marriage almost ended and I almost walked out on everything. If you only knew the pain and torment you would understand that there is no way that I could tell you that any part of this journey has been easy. Many of you do know all too well. What I am saying is that because Kara and I were willing to embrace all aspects of ministry, we were able to overcome, in that year, the things that doom the relationship in this kind of situation. Things like bitterness, unforgiveness, and fear. After that there was still pain, but our relationship was secure, and we knew we would make it and could already see that things were better than they had ever been. Glory to God!

So what did I get from God when I went to him to be my counselor? I got an unbelievable amount of love and affection, and using that he walked me through the emotional hurt and pain so gently. God even exposed some ungodliness in me, for example, finding my rock in my wife. He waited until just the right time and brought correction so lovingly and gently. He is just so soft with us when we are in pain. So he walked me through the emotional and also helped me win the spiritual battles as well. I have already provided testimony of that. He brought insight and revelation every step of the way, and the result was healing in a minute fraction of the time man can bring healing.

I am not convinced that after years of man's way a person is totally free anyway. If the spiritual side is never addressed, then the bondage is still intact. I am not talking about simply having a counselor read the Bible to you or giving you godly advice but actual spiritual warfare without which we remain in bondage. Compound the new bondage from a tragic event with the bondage already in us, and we are in a lot of trouble.

How do you attain transformation and freedom in your life and as a result reflect who God is to your spouse? First, you ask God to ignite the desperation in your soul.

Then ask God to reveal the bondage holding you captive and preventing you from reflecting His character.

The next step is repentance. The first thing John The Baptist and Jesus preached was repentance so it must be the place to begin. I'm not talking about "lip-service" here. Repentance means *"a change of mind accompanied by regret and change of conduct, change of mind and heart."* There is power in repentance. When we come before Father (Jehovah) in humility asking for forgiveness and repent, the doors open to the enemy in our lives are slammed shut.

Once the doors have been shut, it's time to command the enemy to get out of our life in the name of Jesus! I would suggest something like this:

In the name of Jesus I bind you spirit of (bondage repented of) and command you to leave me now!

After this it's important to ask the Holy Spirit to fill you up and saturate the places previously held by the enemy. Obedience comes next and is essential for continued freedom. I will warn you that to be obedient means reacting to situations differently than you have in the past and you are not going to like it! Nobody said the road to the Promised Land was easy and the way we are refined is by choosing to change the way we interact with our spouses and people in general.

As God continues to transform our hearts it becomes easier to walk in Godliness but there will still be times that God asks you to do something very uncomfortable. For example, God may ask you to confess sins to your spouse and ask for their forgiveness. Or God might ask to you cut back on your hours at work despite fears that cutting back would put your job in jeopardy. The things He asks us to do are purposeful in refining and molding us into who He longs for us to be. **If we don't**

move forward when we are uncomfortable we will never grow and we will find ourselves in captivity once again. Obedience is to take steps forward trusting that God has our best interests at heart and will never lead us to destruction.

The only way your marriage is going to be healed is to get desperate and deal with the demonic bondage you are in. We all have access to the spiritual authority needed to deal with Satan and his demons. Unfortunately, there are few out there who really understand that authority and how to walk in it. But Jesus gave us all of the power we need to defeat the enemy and be free so let's begin to recognize that power and walk in it!

> I have given you authority to trample on snakes and scorpions and to overcome all the power of the enemy; nothing will harm you.
>
> Luke 10:19 (NIV)

Conclusion

I believe the time has come to wrap this thing up. My prayer is that God spoke to your heart and used this material to do it. I pray you have found new hope and are willing to try one more thing to restore your marriage. I pray that those of you who feel that your marriage is in a good place are willing to say that there is a chance it could be better. I also pray that God used this material to change not only your marriage but to transform your life.

Our marriages are under attack. Satan is trying to destroy us and he is trying to do it through our marriages. It is sad to admit that Satan is getting the best of our marriages today. There is so much brokenness and so much pain. The pain is not going to be healed unless we allow God to transform us. That may mean entertaining theology that we thought was only for the "crazies." I believe that everything I have presented to you has been biblical and falls into alignment with the character of God.

I do not believe that demons are responsible for everything. However, they are responsible for a whole lot more than we give them credit for. The schemes run deep. We have not been fighting a fair fight. We were born behind the eight ball. Demonic oppression rides the coattails of emotional wounds. They kick us when we are down. They will use anything they can to come into our lives. Let's become aware and start to fight back. Let's begin to take back our marriages. Forget the short-term and long-term assignments to improve your marriage and get free.

If you take the plunge, as a couple, and allow God to set you free from the bondage that you have been living in, your marriage will take care of itself. Allow God to transform you, and you will see everything around you begin to change. The love of God will permeate your entire being and flood your house.

You will find you are doing things like acts of service, words of affirmation, gifts, spending lots of time together, and enjoying lots of nonsexual intimate touch, and they are just flowing out of you. It will be hard for you not to do those things.

Let me tell you something else, sexual intimacy will never be the same. It was incredible when my wife and I were set free from captivity. We began to actually "make love." I had never experienced that before. It was amazing and has stayed that way. There is no lust. There are no candles or mood setting or anything environmental. There is nothing wrong with them, but when we are finally able to truly make love, they do not matter. It is an act of worship to our daddy, God.

I want to talk for a little bit about the reasons from Part A. There are some reasons that I think are just unbiblical, for example, "someone to provide for me financially," "because I have to," and "someone to make me feel good about myself." These reasons were not manipulated and twisted by the enemy but the foundations of these reasons are actually straight from the enemy. There are, however, some of the reasons that are valid and have been twisted and manipulated by the enemy so much that we are not honoring God with them.

Looking at the reasons that I think are biblical but twisted by the enemy, here are some things that I can promise you will begin to see if you and your spouse are willing to get free. Your spouse will become much more loyal and dependable. He/she will still not be able to be those things all of the time, but you will notice a drastic improvement. You will begin to learn and really understand what "making love" is all about, and it will blow you away. Your spouse will begin to open up to you intimately. Your spouse will begin to share feelings, fears, and everything else. You will notice that your spouse is becoming transparent and that you are finally beginning to know him/her. You will begin to spend more time together and touch each other a whole lot more. When you say "I miss you," you will really mean it instead of saying it just to be nice. I know, amazing!

When your spouse hurts you, you will be able to truly forgive, release any bitterness, and move on. You will be able to show grace like you never have before. You will begin to see the love your spouse has for you and the love that God has for you just by looking at him/her. That newly reflected love will begin to hit your spirit, and you will not forget it. Your spouse will begin to understand what love really is, and it will not fail. You will begin to trust in love like you never have before because God is love. For the first time, your spouse will become your best friend. Even though it is not possible or godly to put any trust in your spouse, you will begin to understand that living with hope is possible.

You will see your spouse start to transform in all of these ways I have listed, and you will be greatly encouraged. You will see that he/she is walking with God, and that is very encouraging. You will see that he/she has become aware of who the enemy is, and now he/she knows how to fight it. That is also very encouraging. I cannot know for a fact that Kara will never betray me again because Kara is her own person and makes her own decisions. However, I have seen her transform and display everything that I have listed, and that is very encouraging. My hope in Kara is strong, and my trust in the perfect love of God keeps me from fear.

God has been continuing to teach me about trust and what that means. I was talking to a mentor of mine one night, and I was having a rough time. He told me that God spoke to him and told him that later on that same night God was going change my perspective. I said okay. I went home, and there were some things that I needed to talk to Kara about. There were some things I needed to lay down and ask for her forgiveness in hanging on to them. In that time God spoke to me and said, "Jesse, you can trust her because of me." God said, "It is not the old way anymore. She used to be influenced and blown around by the bondage that she was in, but now it is I who am compelling her to righteousness. You can trust her because of who I am in her." So my "trust" is in the Lord that I see in her, and my "hope" is that she continues to be willing to be compelled by righteousness. This is what we have attained, and continue to attain, as we have been willing, and continue to be willing, to allow God to heal us.

Now let's try this on for size. I don't think that anyone would argue that we were made in the image and likeness of God. If we were made in the image and likeness of God, doesn't that mean that we are, at our core being, holy, pure, worthy, righteous, and trustworthy? We would all agree that God is all of those, so if we were made in his image and likeness, then this would make sense, right? I believe that we are all, at our core being, those five things I mentioned and more. Not because of anything that we have done or not done but because that is who he shaped us to be before the foundations of the earth. I do not see anything in the Word that tells me that at my core I am not those five things.

Paul says in Colossians 1 that we were alienated in *our own minds*. Alienation is not reality; it's our perception. Unfortunately, that has been our perception our whole lives because even in the womb generational sin and iniquity can affect us. So Satan comes in right at the very beginning of life and begins to warp reality for us. By the time we are adults we are so far away from who God created us to be it is laughable.

So what am I telling you now? Am I telling you that in reality everyone is trustworthy after telling you in chapter two that you cannot trust anyone? Well, I guess so, but let me say it this way: Everyone was originally created trustworthy, but until we reach a point to where we first recognize we are not who God created us to be and second become willing to walk through healing and deliverance from the bondage that keeps our perspectives in lies, we are not very trustworthy. So how much healing and wholeness is required to become trustworthy? To be honest, I don't know, but I know that as you pursue God he will tell you. He told me when my wife was there.

Let me share a vision with you that God gave to me. God started to speak to me one day in the middle of a ministry appointment about colors. God led me to ask the woman what color she saw herself as. Truth is that this woman has been through a lot of healing and many areas of her life have been transformed; however, the particular place God was leading us to, in the appointment, was still dark, scary, and unhealed. The problem is that if any area of your life is "dark" to you, it is going to be very difficult, and I would say impossible, to keep the "darkness" from seeping into every other area of your life. So essentially, this woman still viewed herself as being trapped in "darkness." God spoke to me in that moment and told me that he sees her as white and has always seen her that way. White is representing purity, holiness, worthiness, righteousness, and trustworthiness. The vision that God gave me of how this looks was through his eyes. I saw how God looks down through us and into our spirits. The spirit was white, and there were many colors on top of the white; however, all of the other colors were transparent. Especially the "darkness" was transparent.

God never sees us as anything other than white. He looks through the mess, and every so often he wipes away one of those colors on top of the white. Now what motivates God to wipe away the mess so that only white remains? I was discussing this with a good friend of mine who I minister with, and we came to this conclusion: we are the ones who give God permission to wipe away the mess. As we receive salvation and allow God to come in and break away the bondage of the enemy, he wipes away a little more of the mess on top of our spirits.

Beloved, the responsibility is on us. As we come to understand who we have always been, strongholds will be broken, belief systems that don't line up with the Word will die, lies will be exposed, and we will become so much closer to seeing ourselves, *in our own minds,* in the true reality, which is white.

What does this have to do with trust? Everything, because the closer we get to white, the more understanding we gain about the fact God created us trustworthy. When we can see this in others is the point, I think, we can give them the gift of trust because at that point what you are really trusting is God in them because that's all you can see. When people reach this point, I believe they are being compelled to righteousness by the Holy Spirit. That doesn't mean that this person will never let you down or even betray your trust again. What it does mean is what I said before, that we trust in the God we see through them and hope that they will continue to be willing to be compelled by righteousness.

No longer will the phrase "Keep God in the center of your marriage" be a nice thing to say but with no power to change anything. You will begin to understand God becoming the center of your marriage because God has become the center of you. The bondage is gone, and the Holy Spirit remains. You will begin to want to pray and worship together. People will notice a difference in the both of you and how you relate to each other. You will be a testimony of the magnificence of God individually and in your marriage.

I am not saying that everything is going to be perfect. I am saying that things are going to get great in your marriage and in your life. That does not mean you are never going to get attacked by the enemy, and it does not mean you are not going to fall at times. What it does mean is that when you fall your spouse is going to be able to reflect grace, compassion, love, acceptance, and forgiveness. What it does mean is that you will be able to have peace and joy in any circumstance life throws at you. You will be able to find security in God, and that will be enough for you. That is awesome! Praise God!

There will no longer be any record of wrongs because there will be no bitterness and resentment. First Corinthians 13 is going to take on a whole new meaning to you. You will begin to feel good about yourself and to love yourself because you understand love. It will have nothing to do with your spouse but will have everything to do with God.

You will be able to reflect God to your children, and God will be able to reveal who he is to them through you. That is powerful. God will not just be at the center of your marriage but of your entire family. Amen!

I want to address one issue because I know that some of you are thinking it. What if I am willing to be set free but my spouse is not? That is a hard situation. The most powerful testimonies are the ones that you can see day after day. Allow God to set you free, and you will begin to transform right before your spouse's eyes. Then live that testimony every day. Pray for your spouse and wait to see what God does. God will teach you how to have peace in that situation. I promise you he will. The most important thing is that we are freed from captivity individually so that we can have the relationship with God that we desire to have and that he wants with us. Like I said before, allow God to transform and set you free, and the other things will take care of themselves. A friend of mine working through a situation like this has this to say:

Only after the root issues are exposed and uprooted can the real emotional and spiritual surgery start to happen.

We think if I change then he or she will change. That is not always the case. It takes time, and it is, yes, God's timing, not ours. While the other spouse is in transition of change and even while one or the other seems to be in standstill mode, what happens next? The transition with yourself has to come first.

You cannot change your spouse; only God can. Likewise, you are the only one responsible for falling in love with the one being or person in your life who will never leave you nor forsake you. The one who will mend all broken hearts and one who will cleanse and rebuild your heart from the inside out. He will help you love your spouse through the bad and good. Until your heart is changed and your spiritual life is formed into a love relationship with the King of kings and the Lord of lords your marriage is as good as dead because you model with God what you intend on modeling with your spouse. If you spend time with the Father in prayer (releasing to him your downfalls, weaknesses, and concerns), God can then go after your spouse because you have taken yourself out of the physical battle and put yourself on a spiritual battle. God is just waiting for us to stop trying to take his job in most cases.

Look at it this way, if you have a love affair with God and you are totally relying on God for everything you need, there will be no pressure on your spouse to do anything but sit back and watch you grow, hard as it may seem because you do not see your spouse changing at this time. Pretty soon that spouse will become eager to have what you have and to know what you know. That hunger will come only from God. We try too hard sometimes to be the Holy Spirit in our spouses lives. We cannot be that; it is not our job to convict, to soften their hearts, or to change them. That is our Father God s job.

When you've gone through all of the twenty-five steps on how to have a good marriage, found out their love language, left them notes on how they can be a better husband or wife to you, realize this—it only takes one step to get on your knees and cry out to God to change yourself and repent for what hardships you may have caused and then let it go and let God do the rest. It's time to take responsibility for our lives with Christ, and what we do in our own closets will eventually show up in our marriage relationship. He is in the restoration business.

Beloved, Jesus said that he has come so that we can have life in abundance. I am finished with the bondage of misery, pain, and suffering. I am sure that in the time I have left in this world I will experience more pain and suffering, but I am finished with the bondage, and with the help of God, I will stay finished. I am ready to move into joy, peace, and love. I am finished with being a slave to the enemy, and I am ready to be a slave to God. Let's allow God to set us free and start to take back our lives from the clutches of the enemy. God bless!

Contact Information

If you would like to contact Jesse and Kara e-mail your request and contact information to reflectministry@yahoo.com. If you would like Jesse and Kara to come to your church or facility as guest speakers, e-mail your information to reflectministry@yahoo.com.

> We accept man's testimony, but God's testimony is greater because it is the testimony of God, which he has given about his Son.
>
> 1 John 5:9

If God has used this book to help you in any way, we want to hear your testimony. Testimonies bless the body of Christ, and we want everyone to hear about how God is moving in our lives. Testimonies encourage, comfort, and exhort. If you would like to share your testimony, send it to us at reflectministry@yahoo.com.

Visit us on the Internet at www.marriagewhatsthepoint.com. There you will find book information, book ordering information, author information, seminar schedule, testimonies all about the power of God, and more. Also visit our Facebook fan page titled "Marriage What's the Point?"

Bibliography

American Pregnancy. "American pregnancy.org." 2000–2009.

http://www.americanpregnancy.org

Catalogs.com. "Catalogs.com: Percentage of people who cheat." 1997–2009.

http://www.catalogs.com/info/relationships/percentage-of-married-couples-who-cheat-on-each-ot.html

Chapman, Gary. *Toward a Growing Marriage.* Self-published. 1979, 1996.

CNN. "CNN.com." Turner Broadcasting System Inc. 2010.

http://www.cnn.com/

Divorce Magazine. "DivorceMagazine.com." Jeffrey Cottrill. 2009.

http://www.divorcemag.com/

Electronic Sword "E-Sword." Rick Meyers. 2009.

http://www.e-sword.com

I Love Quotes.com. "1-Love-Quotes.com." Top ten user-rated love quotes of all time. 2008.

http://www.1-love-quotes.com/Top_10_Love_Quotes.htm

Kids Health. "Kidshealth.org." 1995–2009.

http://www.kidshealth.org

Newsweek. "Newsweek.com." Newsweek Inc. 2010.

http://www.newsweek.com/

Professorhouse. "Professorhouse.com."

http://www.professorhouse.com/

Softpedia. "news.softpedia.com." 2001–2010.

http://news.softpedia.com/

Webster's dictionary. "Merriam-webster.com." Fred Mish. 2009. http://www.merriam-webster.com

Wright, Henry. *A More Excellent Way.* Whitaker House. 1999.

Yahoo. "Yahoo answers: Opinions on marriage." Yahoo. 2009. http://answers.yahoo.com/question/index?qid=20061126042329 AALekbz

Yahoo. "Yahoo answers: Opinions on being alone." Yahoo. 2009. http://answers.yahoo.com/question/index?qid=20061126042329 AALekbz

.